DR. DAVID R. L. STEVENS

Parenting

Equipping Babies For A Lifetime

Vol. 3

PARENTING:
EQUIPPING BABIES FOR A LIFETIME

Copyright © 2025 **Dr. David R. L. Stevens**

ISBN (Paperback): 979-8-89672-248-9
ISBN (Hardback): 979-8-89672-250-2
ISBN (Ebook): 979-8-89672-249-6

Printed in the United States of America.

PROMINENT
BOOKS
EDGE

5830 E 2nd St, Ste 7000 #9983
Casper, WY 82609
USA

Contents

Dedication

Again, I dedicate this work to God and His church, and then, to the memory of my beautiful, devoted wife Dorothy, who was suddenly called home 9/12/2025 by the Master. Dot was my cherished rock and special angel for 63 years and 4 days. It is so hard to imagine life without her. Very seldom were we ever apart. Everything was done together. I know that she would urge me to continue writing books and trying to help people find the joy and love we shared. So, I'll say to the departed love of my life, *"Dorothy, by the grace of God, I'll keep plugging along until that great day when we meet again on heaven's shores"*.

Special recognition to our four children and their spouses, Mike & Becky, Shana, still my editor extraordinaire & Brian, Faith & Russell, and David & Robin, who are all involved in kingdom work. Now you know I'm not going to leave out our ten grandchildren by age: Michael, Timothy, Daniel, Joshua, Imani, Sarah, David Kweli, Nyla, Nia, and Solomon Kabisa. Also, this is the first book that I get to introduce our two great-grandchildren, Christian and Fawn, and the baby on the way. What a wonderful growing dynasty in the making! Thank you, Christ Center Church of God, for sharing us with the world at large. You've allowed us to go and serve others in seminars and workshops without complaint. In those times when I needed time to write, you were most gracious, even when we took a partial sabbatical that was not on anyone's radar. I am truly blessed to have such a great congregation of loving, caring people. Thank you again for not placing too many extra demands on our time. You have grasped the understanding that God has not only sent us to serve you, but a larger world as well, and we love you with our lives! Then there is my special staff: Pastors Elsa Johnson Bass, Vera H. Odum, Brian Boykin, David Scott Owens III., Co, and Cornelius Bolger, who, with my Administrative Assistant Ms. Beverly J. Adams, continue to make me look good. Thank you so much for all your dedicated work. May God continue to bless you and your families as you serve the Kingdom.

Foreword

This is the seventh book in this series on relationships. The previous book is really two books in one. LOVE and MARRIAGE For A LIFETIME promotes understanding each discipline. LOVE, Vol. 1, centers on the dating process as foundational to what follows. MARRIAGE FOR A LIFETIME, Vol. 2, moves from the altar to the bedroom and beyond. This is the wisdom that produces winners.

We now add a requested look at the important task of having children. PARENTING: EQUIPPING BABIES FOR A LIFETIME provides a helpful contemporary guide to working with children. Some things have changed since raising our children, but we strongly believe that Biblical principles do not change but applications may. I continue to be fascinated by the way God has set His principles to bless us. Searching out this wisdom continues to be a lifelong journey. The Bible is God's WORD, why would we not want to follow it? One researcher actually counted over 8,000 promises in the Bible. While there certainly are many of these promises directed toward us as individuals, there is a plethora of them directed toward the family. Personally, I need every blessing that was designed for me and my family. Again, in this book I've tried to pull out wisdom that continues to help those wise enough to seek it. I have included many real-life accounts that help bring focus to principles. For it is in following principles that we gain the highest and richest blessings. Judge Joan Barnes Perry-Stewart said, *"Everybody needs this information! Smart, not so smart, single, couples . . .. EVERYBODY"*! We do agree, and hope that parents read this collection of wisdom gleaned from the wisdom that **The Marriage Maker** provides. We also recommend that where possible, spouses read, study, and discuss a chapter together. You will find this book helpful for discussion groups, with single, married, and divorced parents. We believe that biblical principles always work. However, because of one's culture, tradition and maybe sometimes a particular lifestyle some principles are more adaptable than others, or it may take a longer time to understand the application. Remember however, some flexibility does not mean avoiding, ignoring, or rejecting a principle. Please enjoy this latest effort; it is intended to be simple and easy to understand yet yielding an impactful surge in your relationship energy. Knowledge is power. Power to understand, and power to activate that understanding. Practicing these truths will lead to a greater life. Once again, I give to you over fifty years of personal experience and passionate study.

BEFORE MAKING BABIES!

L et's be real. You're not going to find many devout church-people talking outwardly about sex! It's like some kind of secret that everybody knows about, but mums the word. In the church we will discuss almost anything, yeah but not sex. It's quite hilarious when little children ask where babies come from watching some church members try to make up explanations. Back in the day a popular explanation was that the stork brought them to the house. More precocious children wanted to know how storks read addresses, got into the house, and found the nursery room? It was so amusing to hear parents making up clandestine answers. Of course, Christians don't lie!

Unfortunately, on top of everything else there is still a misguided population that feels intercourse was only invented so that people could have children. No, intercourse can be a pathway to having children, however, it was designed with a much weightier importance. Actually, The Marriage Act (sex) was meant to preclude having children. Before God talked about humans being fruitful and multiplying, God was concerned about establishing the institutional state of a man joining a woman in what we call marriage.

1

Marriage, according to Genesis 2:24, is built on three basic principles: 1. Two people permanently **Leaving** former family structures that they formally leaned on for support, in exchange for a new exclusive system. 2. Publicly now declaring to **Cleave** to this new dual alliance that spiritually, socially, and physically becomes mysteriously, a single- alliance, and 3. Becoming again mysteriously, **One Flesh**, spouse to spouse relationship! This is God's mathematical system 1 + 1 = 1!

Over and over, and over again I have found that it's not about understanding God's system and how it works, but If we trust God and His system the onus is on Him. He makes it work!

One flesh is the biblical description for sex. It is not trying to be a clinical, or scientific term, but very accurately sums up the function. When the life- producing organs connect, oneness is expressed! Complete beauty of this oneness is experienced when the other two elements are a part of God's threefold plan. Then God's commitment to us is realized when we follow that plan. God honors our commitment by making it all work!

Okay I said let's be real! Sex was invented by God to give great pleasure to married folks! Married folks reap the promises of God. Sorry, the promise does not cover unmarried folks. The sex might be good, but the promised fidelity is incomplete. You will not hear that based on world standards, but God did not set up based on what the world wants to practice. You might want to forgive me here, but I am a preacher called by God to tell the truth. Let me get back on track.

Making babies is extremely important, but it is a byproduct of sexual intimacy. It's not dirty, shameful, unholy or inappropriate. It is regular, normal and **EXPECTED**! The reason I am making this point is that there is an alarming number of couples that are neglecting this third element of God's designed thinking it to be unnecessary other than making a family. No, it was invented to be 1/3 of the marriage contract. It is so important that if neglected the other two elements are likely to fall prey to eventual erosion.

Let me share from my earlier book **MARRIAGE: CATCHING A SECOUND WIND** 2010:

Gerard and his wife have not been sexually intimate for over a decade. Interestingly, just like they don't deal with each other sexually, they don't deal with each other in any other area either. Kelly and Sam have gone almost 15 years without having intercourse after the birth of their third daughter. Their relationship is about as bad as it can get. While Gerard and Diane ignore each other, Kelly and Sam choose to yell violently at each other all the time. Then there is the example of Patricia and Charles who engage in sex maybe every three or four months, providing that they are not mad with each other at the time. We need to be careful to recognize that every marriage where sexual intimacy is not being regularly practiced is not necessarily one where they are sniping at each other. For a while they may get along, but watch out, don't take it lightly. This kind of behavior is certain to be a love killer. Rarely, if ever, do you find couples that avoid each other sexually, in a great love place. When intimacy is missing over an extended period of time, the couple will not tell you honestly that they are happy in love. No-sex at this point usually represents an ugly impasse that will lead to certain destruction in the relationship. Remember these couples probably did not plan this separation at first but it gets easier and easier down the road. There are some marriages managing to go along on an empty love tank, without bitterness at first, but trust me the storm is coming. There are usually two noted responses to a missing pattern of sexual intimacy. It will show up as cool indifference or volatile rage. This may be the point at which divorce enters in. Ernest and Joan tend to ignore each other with cool indifference. They would explain it as being too old to care about that part of their lives. That's an interesting excuse, but why the noted indifference toward each other? Then what about that statement: *"We are too old to care"*? Is there any age limit?

Actually, if we trust biblical mandate, we find that sex involves one third of the covenantal marriage makeup and it does not say anything about an age limit. If you look at the history of Abraham and Sarah, how was she able to give birth at age 90? The age was amazing, of course, but this means they must have been having sex all along. Sexual intercourse wasn't only to produce children but as a natural marital relationship practice. Oh, and just for the record, did you know that after Sarah died at the age of 127, Abraham was then around 137, and he got married again? That's right he married Katurah, and they had 6 children over a period of 38 years. Not too shabby old Abe! **Reader, *I need to SMILE for you!* (*Several noted Jewish historians have concluded from their research that Hagar and Katurah were the same person.)* I have been teaching for many years what I call The Triangular Plan, based on the writings of Walter Trobish. This plan is also found in Genesis, the first book of the Bible, Chapter 2, verse 24. The scriptural formula divides marriage into three specific sections or actions. It mentions Leaving, as the public lawful separation from parents and others as a first step. We see this being acted out in the marriage ceremony as the father leaves the bride in the care of the groom at the altar. Next the passage of Scripture instructs that Cleaving is the vowing of an emotional and/or physical commitment to love and fidelity. Then there is that interesting term, "One flesh" that finalizes the covenant. One flesh is the exclusive spiritual, physical, and mental relational factor shared with a married partner. It takes these three elements to have a legitimate consummated marriage. Most religious weddings have some form of following these procedures. I suggest looking at the Gen.2:24 passage which is where I derive my illustration of a three-legged stool that is like the whole foundation of a marriage. For the stool to stand, it must have each of its legs planted squarely on the ground. If a leg is removed, the stool will fall on the ground.

I am certainly not trying to make any of the legs more important than the others. They are all important. Yet they must all be there to do the job as intended. I am pretty convinced that in a great many of the cases I have observed over the years, where there is long-term marital conflict, sexual intimacy is either completely missing, or it is practiced so slightly that it might as well be missing. I can understand why people in troubled marital conditions don't feel like being intimate. Even if they were having sex physically, it certainly is not going to be in any way intimate. True intimacy taps into the mental, emotional, and spiritual, as well as the physical.

It is a well-known fact that anger will steal the joy from intimacy. Yet on the other hand I believe that there are many married couples who are not particularly upset with each other but have carelessly adopted a no sex-or little sex mentality! Warning: this usually will become cool indifference which is another form of rage or volatile rage itself. Whether volatile or cool, the results are the same. They are both love killers. (***Please note we are not talking about where there is a physical or mental situation where sexual intimacy would be inappropriate***.)

If sex is to be clearly understood from the Genesis 2:24 passage, then it's place of importance is one third of the marriage equation. Just as the other two tenets of the marriage triangle need to be regularly practiced, the one flesh relationship that Dr. Tim LaHaye calls "The Marriage Act," must also be regularly practiced.

There are all kinds of theories about how many times, and how often is normal sexual activity? If there was a "Normal," it would set the bar for everyone to follow. What might be even "Normal" for a couple in their first 10 years may increase or decrease in their next 10 years. Who can predict? So, setting an average normal number of times a couple should have intercourse is not possible, because people are varied individuals. Each couple has their own unique chemistry. I can imagine if we could give a factual number of times that sexual intercourse should be practiced in a marital context, it would only provide another point for specific groups of analysts to fight over. No, actually, the bar is set by a married couple's private decisions. It is up to them exclusively, as long as it does not fall into the realm of being ridiculously sparse or absent. Ridiculous (ruling out illness, etc.) is for a married couple living in the same space to go weeks and months at a time without engaging in the Marriage Act because they refuse to deal with solvable issues etc. Again, we can agree upfront that if they live in different cities because of work, etc., and can only get together when time and distance permits, this does not count as an intentional violation. Any situations of an unusual nature are excluded from this conversation. The funny thing here is that these are not usually the people having the problems of inconsistency. They seem to have no problem working it out. I once heard the story of a famous jet-set couple who lived on two different coasts. They said, "We plan our get-togethers as being great celebrations. When we get together it is always shooting stars and Roman candles.

Sex definitely does matter in the marital life of the contented. In God's design, sexual intimacy helps to bring about contentment. Just as we have pointed out in the book Marriage: The Rules of the Game, 'sex is not love, and love is not sex,' but they do act to support each other. My concern for sexual intimacy is directed more toward a couple's pattern regularity. This is not based so much on the number of times, but more on the regularity or irregularity. We understand that things happen. This may alter times, but if we look more at the pattern of things it would give a better picture of the couples' intimate health. Again, we take a look at what the Marriage Makers' book says on the subject. 1. Corinthians 7:5 says, *"Do not deprive one another except with consent for a time that you may give yourselves to fasting and prayer; and come together again so that Satan does not tempt you because of your lack of self-control."*

Notice the key phrases that stick out: 1. Do not deprive (sexually) 2. Except with consent 3. For a time 4. (for) prayer and fasting 5. (in order to) come together again (sexually) 6. (so that) Satan does not tempt you (while you are not being intimate). The scripture is pointing out clearly that when we are fasting, we are not to engage in sexual exploits of any kind. However, let's not forget the strong scriptural implication here, is that there should be an agreement before entering into a period of fasting as well as a reasonable time limit. A husband or a wife should not decide independently one day, *"I'm going to fast."* Nor should they set a long-term date that is unreasonable. There has to be an agreement that is practical and beneficial. The Marriage Maker's book says that *his body belongs to her, and her body belongs to him.* There can't be an, *"Oh baby, didn't I tell you I'll be fasting for the next 60 days?"* you would be working against scripture. Remember in that scripture it tells us to make it brief (see v.5 *"for a time"*). Now I know that the more holy among us are going to differ with me because fasting is a very spiritual thing that is God honoring. How dare I suggest that intimacy takes precedence over fasting? I'm sorry but let the word speak for itself. Read again carefully 1 Corinthians 7:5 for yourself: *5Do not deprive one another except with consent for a time that you may give yourselves to fasting and prayer; and come together again so that Satan does not tempt you because of your lack of self-control. Then read verses 3 and 4 to gain the context: 3Let the husband render to his wife the affection due to her, and likewise also the wife to her husband. 4The wife does not have authority over her own body, but the husband does. And likewise, the husband does not have authority over his own body, but the wife does.* I rest my case!

There is that occasional time when a spouse just may not be able to perform. This is to be expected in the life of human beings. My concern centers on the normal times when a couple could be and should be intimate. The point is if you are married to each other, you cannot arbitrarily decide not to be intimate with each other. That's sin! Causing an argument to avoid being sexually intimate, as is practiced by some, is sin also! Once again, to make the point from another angle, to do these rebellious acts to avoid expressing intimacy is sin, according to the Bible the Marriage Manual!

We do need to spend some time talking to those spouses who do have some genuine sexual challenges. What if you are unable to function in this area of your marriage? First, we need to affirm that there is no sin here. If there is a problem of physical discomfort, we are fortunate to be living in times of great medical enlightenment. I believe that God has invested a great amount of ever-increasing knowledge into the mind banks of medical practitioners. I also believe that if you are facing sexual challenges there are expert physicians out there who can help you. Don't you and your spouse suffer in silence?

Please do not give up. Help can be on the way. If God has given us this beautiful gift, it is unlikely that He would not supply the answer to our problems. Yet it is incumbent upon us to do everything in our power to find a cure. Don't give up, don't give in! Seek diligently for God's way! God has given us this incredible gift of sexual intimacy; He must have a way for us to fulfill that gift. It starts with prayer!

I know a lot of religious people don't understand it, or believe it, but sex was placed there by God and placed there for a reason. God planned it that way from the beginning. Ignore it and it has the power to destroy a marital relationship. Work with it and it has the power to bring health, healing, and contentment. It keeps the flow going in the marital relationship. When I urged Jameson and Amy to make sexual intimacy a regular part of their relationship, they began to see a new level of harmony sprouting. Sex took the edge off of their marriage issues. Arguments began to lessen and practically disappear. Once the enjoyment of totally loving each other caught on, they seemed not to be able to keep their hands off of each other. After I learned they followed this advice, I didn't want to call them and certainly did not want to visit them. It was very likely they were spending a lot of private time, doing who knows what. (smiles!) **They went from zero to full tilt, on this one!**

Now understand, I'm not saying that sex is the most important thing in the marriage relationship. What I am saying is that it is so important that it should not be neglected. Children are an added blessing to the married couple. But do not place the value of the relationship on having children. If your relationship does not produce offspring, then God has other ways for you to serve Him. There is no doubt that He has other ways for you to be fruitful and multiply in the Kingdom of God. **Find that purpose together while appreciating the gift that He has given.**

PARENTING THE
ADDED BLESSING

Often God chooses to bring children into the lives of a married couple. Actually, more often than not! A childless couple however should realize that marriage itself is a tremendous blessing. The blending of two hearts into one is a great miracle. Jesus chose to begin His series of great miracles in Cana of Galilee at a wedding feast.

Everyone is familiar with that great miracle that came after they ran out of wedding wine. Mary, Jesus' Mom approached Him to help out the hosts by not letting them suffer social embarrassment. To throw a feast and not have enough provisions was regarded as a social faux pas. Remember in those times wedding celebrations could last for several days. To save the day Jesus had the waiters fill two gigantic urns with water. Then He turned that water into genuine wine. The guests were amazed at the new wine coming from the kitchen because it was towards the end of the celebration. What would have been sheer embarrassment for the hosts turned into a greater achievement because they said that this later wine was not what they were expecting. It was actually superior to what had been served all night. The usual pattern was that after everyone had their fill, those hosting would bring out the cheap stuff. Jesus took the time and effort to turn a near social tragedy into a huge triumph. This is how much God favors matrimony by itself. Marriage done right is a blessing. When He allows children to come into that relationship it is an added blessing. Your first and greatest blessing is the two of you. Never allow children to come between you or dull your love relationship. This word is especially to moms. Never allow the love you have for your husband to be displaced, or put on hold because of the children. So many marriages have suffered because the children were allowed to get in the way. Love them, but make them to know that they come second to your spouse. That's the glue that holds families together!

The Biggggggg Question . . .

Why does God give children to some and not to others? This is something we cannot answer. Not being able to have children is certainly not based on worthiness. I've known couples that were excellent in character. Actually more excellent than some whom we really question why they had children. It can't be based on a couple's ability to financially provide; we all know families who are very poor but have a wealth of children. Health is not always an issue either. There are many stories of mothers giving birth with high odds given for them not making it through the pregnancy; yet they did survive and some of them went on to deliver again. So why, and what makes the difference in having children? Simply put, we must leave it up to the sovereignty of God. He does what He wants to, just like He wants to, and that's our best answer. But this I know, that the union of a man and a woman in marriage is no small blessing because it is highly sanctioned by God, with or without children!

Many years ago, I heard Christian Psychologist Dr. James Dobson share an interesting observation. He said that over the years he knew many couples who after they had been years without children decided to adopt one. He chuckled with his radio co-host as he revealed that right after the adoption, guess what? The woman became pregnant! *"Over and over"* Dr. Dobson said he had observed this phenomenon happening. He wondered, tongue in cheek, if this was not the fool—proof way to open up the birth canal. Although we have also heard of this happening, I would not want to count too heavily on this being the magic seeding method. However, adoption does prove to be the answer for many previously childless couples. Many others have taken on the supportive roles of godparents, or play-parents, guardians, etc. The task being so great today many parents appreciate an extra set of caregivers.

Great care of course needs to be taken not to go over boundaries. In this latter group it would be well to remember that you are not the parent but in support of the parent. When the parents establish a rule don't take it upon yourself to disregard that rule. You may disregard yourself out of a relationship. Dana-Marie had the care of Susan and Girard's two little guys. They had a no sugar policy going that Dana-Marie was well aware of. She said to the children, *"In my house everyone gets rewarded with some candy." "A little candy never hurts anyone."* Well, that proved to not be true. The parents found out that she persisted in doing what they had asked her not to do. Dana-Marie continued to cross the line, so they terminated their relationship with her.

I try to remind new parents when they are in the process of selecting a godparent to choose someone that will have a like-mind in helping to raise their children. The selection process for couples today is more ceremonial. These choices are usually based on friendship alone. Friendship is good but to be wise is to spend some time praying and looking into the philosophical and theological positions of the candidate. It is wonderful that you are friends and that you love each other, but remember you are seeking someone who shares your way of life and how you want your child to grow up.

The Melendez family were Christians with a real passion for the church. They were considering asking their next door neighbors the Shiasabey's who were worshipers in a totally different religious system to be godparents to their son. Pharsee and Delia Shiasabey loved little Tony and his family and were fine folks, but this was not a good idea. They believed differently. This kind of decision cannot be based on love alone. If God has not blessed you through a pregnancy before going on to some other method of becoming a parent you should do some healthy self-examination. See if you have the traits and qualities needed to become a parent. Here are some helpful questions to be considered in answering that question.

First check your tolerance level:
- Are you easily upset by noises generated by others?
- What is your likely reaction to stinky diapers?
- Are you willing to listen to endless conversation coming from a child's worldview?
- Can you recover from the Messies; crayon marks, Jell-O spills, Magic markers gone wild?
- How about putting up with children's clutter?
- Toddler's dinners graciously shared with the floor?
- Endless distress calls in the night?
- Unexpected bed visits just when you had dropped off or are sharing private moments?
- Slip—and—falls caused by toys in the strangest places?
- Silly squabbles between (the child and your spouse)?

Then check your sacrifice level:
-	You have saved money to get a special tool/appliance but school clothes are needed.
-	You want to put more time into finishing a work project but attendance at a school play is expected.
-	Music, dance, and acting lessons take precedence over family vacations.
-	College completion, or career plans put on hold in order to advance your children and their financial needs.

Being a parent certainly calls for tolerance and many sacrifices. Enter into it with your eyes open and focused on the prize. The prize comes when you have done a good job and as it says in Proverbs 31 "... *your children rise up and call you blessed*". Smile, it may take awhile! Try as you may you will not always get it right. You will make some mistakes along the road but if you follow the plan the end result will be good.

Don't force the issue!

Gaston and Eugenia O'Hennesee knew that they wanted a child, but after trying for several years, and some serious medical test results, it became pretty conclusive that this pregnancy would not be happening; at least not by natural birth. Out of impatience and frustration they decided to adopt. It turned out that God was right all along! They were terrible parents! Gaston had a terrible temper and very little patience. There were times that he literally dared their daughter to breathe. Eugenia did not help matters because she would always verbally blame Gaston and say it was her husband's fault for making this adoption arrangement. They were crazy and just about drove their child nuts too. What an environment to grow up in. You wake up in the morning and find that your parents are already disgusted with you because you snored last night; or their total frustration because of making you breakfast this morning. This is the way she had to grow up. Almost, never a kind word; complaints and ridicule just about every day. She could do absolutely nothing right. In school she could not cope because of her lack of self-confidence. She got through who knows how? It just was one unfortunate dilemma.

Thank God and God alone that the life of this precious young woman was not lost. God pulled her through and gave her meaning and purpose. To this day there is a separation in this family. I'm not sure that this is a bad thing for this young lady's sake. Laura will continue to do well on her own not having to listen to the hateful criticism of these misfit parents. May I say one more time, *"God was right all along"*!

This of course is an extreme example and does not reflect on the reason most childless couples are so. This story is about one husband and one wife that decided that they would remove all odds to have their way no matter what God said. This kind of belligerent attitude that drives rebellious actions will never turn out to be a good thing.

It was a delight to watch Gene and Irma Dixon raise their adopted son. I don't think he ever felt any way other than these were his natural parents. Even when he learned that he had been adopted by the Dixons because his biological mom had no means of taking care of him without the help of a husband. It seemed to make no difference in how he felt. They loved him, disciplined him, and cared for him with that great love that parents give when they are being truly led from above. I'm not sure where they got all of their training. Neither of them finished high school. But they seemed to be naturally good parents who had a lot of wisdom. Irma would tell you that she prayed her way through and that God would give her a lot of insight. Gene was very quiet but set much of the pace for the family. If he said "no" then that was the answer. Their son was raised up in the church with no choice of anything else. He didn't get an alternative vote. Some parents now like to leave it up to the child. I know a momma right now who likes to leave church going up to her little daughter who more often than not chooses to stay home or go to some of her girlfriends' houses. In the Dixon household every human walking had to go to church on the Lord's Day. That was policy! This was pretty much how I was raised up, how my wife was raised up, and how we raised up our children.

This policy did not hurt us one bit and we are all still following this same practice. I've shared with our congregation often, how much this was so engrained in me. When I was about 16 going on 17 years old, I was trying to establish a career in baseball. Our team was in a semi-pro league that scheduled Sunday games. I would drive to church first for service and then bolt out afterwards putting my uniform on as I drove to where the game was. Most of the time I would make it just in time to toss a few warm up balls before the game. No, I was not trying to be *"saved"*; it was just something I needed to do! It was in me!

After High school I deliberately went far away to college. (*Actually, it was God's plan; I didn't know it at the time.*) I did it, I thought, so that I could be on my own. But interestingly I went to church every Sunday on my own anyway. The funny thing looking back now is that, still not even being *"saved"*, I went to many of the mid-week services too. The church habit was in me! So, when God got a hold of me for real, that was not one of the things He had to deal with me about. Certainly there were others! *Parents put church in your children's present and future!* It will help them; never hurt them. This is a strong principle. We have seen it work first hand, over and over again in our family, and in the lives of other families.

PARENTING BY HERSELF

Alice Johansson is a wonderful mother. I watched her almost single handedly raise her sons with integrity. She taught them God first family next and your church family after that. She taught them not to bury their heads in the sand when it came to world affairs, politics, and social justice and its issues. She taught them further that the first three things mattered the most and would give them proper perspective to all the rest of life. I say she raised them *"almost"* single handedly because she did have help. She was wise enough to look out on her dilemma and decide it really does take a village to raise a child. She immediately set out on an enlistment campaign in the church. From the Janitor to the C.E. O. if you were a responsible male, you had an assignment!

Alice was devastated with what seemed like an abrupt betrayal and abandonment by her husband. She later found out that her discovery may have been sudden but that his unfaithfulness went several years back. We don't know if the abandonment was planned or unplanned, but when the truth of his adultery surfaced he was gone. What in the world was she to do with two babies all by herself?

Now I have heard silly women make ridiculous claims that they, *"... don't need no man"*; and *"I can be their mother and father"* and so on! Ridiculous, ridiculous! If you are a mother alone in the parenting role I understand the challenges you face and each triumph is a victory! But don't get pumped! Denial of the importance of a strong father figure is not going to make the journey easier. You do need, not just a man, but many strong men helping to set an example for your children. I am not speaking of a romantic connection here at all. This is strictly parental business. The first source should be the natural father if he is around, and capable. In many cases, this is not a factor because many fathers when they take off from the marriage feel free to gallop. This was true with Alice's ex. He took off on his own sordid journey. I admit to a personal bias here: I do not recommend divorce if there is any outside chance of saving a marriage; however, if your man cuts and runs leaving his children behind, as casualties, I think you should take him for all that he is worth and then some! Don't settle too quickly either! Search out every bank account, stock holding, and investment he even thought about having. No, don't *"Pastor"* me, as if I just hit you with a hot plate of grits. The Bible says that a man that refuses to take (*proper*) care of his family is worse than a heathen.

Listen heathen! If you are reading this, I have no sympathy for you. *Take care of your kids* and then we can talk. Ok, ok, I'll settle down now and get back to land. Understand, there are a few things that push me across the line. Because Alice saw the importance of bringing some strong godly men into the lives of her sons these now young men have grown up strong and are teaching those same principles. Both of them have become world changers for sure. What was the secret of Alice's method? No secret, she found it right in the Bible, *"Train up a child in the way he should go, and when he gets old, he will not depart from that training"*. Alice learned that there are two outstanding parts to that Proverbs 22:6 training assignment. Often the spiritual community will gravitate to the first and sometimes stumble over the second. The first part is certainly the spiritual mandate to bring children up bathed in the scriptural structures and attributes of the word. That is important! But of equal importance is training that child, those children up according to their temperament and character.

I get to watch two sets of grand children being raised up. Five of them are being pretty much raised together. They are more like sisters and brothers than cousins. What I observe is that in spite of their closeness they are each different in temperament, character, and personality. In one of the households there are two sisters; years apart but both raised the same way. I noticed that some of the things that were done with the older child, who is more compliant, just will not work with the other girl. Sweet as she is, often it looks like her mind was made up way before she came here to earth that she was not going to do what you asked her to do.

I notice that her daddy has to take her to another part of the room and softly remind her, what she will, or will not do. She will come back and reluctantly give a weak *"I'm sorry"*, but probably not promise that there will be no repeat performance someday, maybe even that same day.

In the other family, their middle child, a girl, will hardly tell you, *"No, I won't go"*! She will give you the prettiest smile and look at you with her beautiful eyes and refuse to change behavior. Her daddy taking her to the other side of the room to speak softly to her would be as affective as me putting pennies in a quarter parking meter. I would be putting money in technically, but what I was putting in would not move the dials of the meter. I get to watch these two very fine fathers working affectively with their children. Each of them I know is praying as they work with these precious five gifts God has given.

Now in sharing the above, I've also noticed that both men are not only there to step in when their wives are exasperated but are actively involved in the day to day management. These families have worked out this parents-as-partner thing pretty well. They indeed need each other! So, training children successfully does require both parts of this principle. Put in them all the spiritual stuff you can, but remember to look for and work with, and sometimes on, the individual makeup of that child. Alice and thousands of other mothers have learned the value of the God-centered village. There are things learned in this community that cannot be learned or experienced anywhere else. When the citizens of this community correctly practice the principles found in the Bible they find that their success rate is far higher than those following a man-made system, or an uncharted series of guesses.

In our present society many people are very uncomfortable with the Bible admonition to physically correct one's children. In all fairness it is not telling a parent to abuse a child. It only says that if you fail to teach discipline to your children you are setting the stage for their demise. Back in the day, as some say, the good folks at church would make themselves part of the discipline committee. These members thought nothing about stepping up alongside of a church youth and issuing some verbal rebukes along with some threats of laying on hands. Most of the youth back then did not challenge these pseudo parents because they seemed a little mental and might just try to follow through on the threats. Then on top of that, the even more mentally challenged parents, who often promised to issue out a second dose of physical correction. So, it was just better to behave one's self and try to go along with these unstable parental police-types. The interesting thing though, the numbers of children, *'back in the day'*, matriculating into the respectable sectors of society seemed to be much higher. It seems that the more rigid, but loving discipline did work, and worked well. The jail systems were not overloaded!

Again, a parent must learn their child. The same kind of punishment or discipline measures will not work with every child the same way. The key is in helping the child to learn what is right and what is not right.

In order to teach a child what hot is, you do not put the child in real danger. Yet you have to make it real enough that the child identifies hot with possible pain and danger. Spanking does not always work either. You have to exercise wisdom in your discipline. We found that spanking was not always the most effective way to deal with one of our gems. We had to find a way to mix up the punishment so that that child would never know what was coming. Trying to figure out the consequences became so bothersome that often the misbehavior was not worth the effort. I laugh at that offspring who these days is challenged with some children that now cause them some prayers for the gift of creative punishment. Oh, I'm not sure the Bible would put it that way, but I think you get the point.

Be consistent in your expectations. Do not feel one way one time and change up another time. Your children need you to be consistent with them. They become confused when parents don't hold a steady line. If you find that you need to change a previously held stand, you can do this with careful communication. Let your child know that you felt that a certain behavior warranted a particular punishment, but that now after thinking about it you feel that it calls for a new consequence. This could be less or more. The most effective timing for this discussion is before the infraction. Don't wait until the infraction to announce a change in policy.

In keeping with the village concept of raising a child, especially with a single mom, try consulting with your village when looking for ways to discipline. You want to consult with the most responsible and balanced individuals you can find. Avoid those people who are extreme in their views of punishment. Some from the too liberal side might suggest for any infraction sitting down and reasoning with your young rule breaker, or sending them to time out for all bad behavior. These are valid methods of correction in their proper place. Then on the other end of disciplinarians are those that feel you need to spank for everything. You want to talk to folks who are kind of in the middle-people. People, who are willing to look at various infractions and develop strategies of how to discipline. They are not so liberal that anything goes, nor are they spank crazy.

Be careful that you don't give too detailed of an account that will bring unwarranted shame later to the child. Unless it is so needed, try being more general as you consult with your village. You would hate for your now grown-offspring to have someone bring up something from the past that embarrasses, or negatively labels them.

Jonnie tried to raise her children without the help of the village. She had several children by the same man who never wanted to marry her. He was not altogether absent from their lives but was not really around for the day to day. He would do the visitation thing on occasion but she pretty much tried to rear them on her own. She worked hard to supply their needs but it was a real struggle. To her, the children could do no wrong. Working extra hours to make ends meet she had to sort of leave them to their own devices. They were not real bad children but they knew how to get over on their mom. Getting over became their game.

Jonnie was so protective of her children that no one could tell her about their behavior. She said on more than one occasion, *"I' ll kill for my kids"*. There was no village for them at her own doing. Her children grew up just like that. They were selfish, ungrateful, spoiled and had little interest in others; including Jonnie. Even today they are not even trying to provide some help for their mom who is still working hard with no relief for her tired bones. All she seems to be to them is a convenient baby sitter and an occasional co-signer for their loans. There were areas that others saw that needed some serious fixing but Jonnie shut the village out!

Direct intervention sometimes helps

Many times, over the years I have been asked as a village member to speak to a child about their bad behavior. These conversations have taken place with children of single parents and children who live with both parents alike. I always remind my young charge that it is a real blessing to have someone who loves you enough to want to check your poor decisions. I remind them that they could be in a situation where no one cares what they do. Most children can understand that this is not a good situation to have no one care.

Sometimes, I use the disappointment card. *"Your mom was so hurt when she discovered that she could not trust you"*. *"It hurt her so much that she felt that she had not done a good job in helping you to be a good person"*. Trust me, no child wants his parent to feel and think that they have failed as a parent. Secondly it cuts to the core when you feel that your parent has lost all trust in you. Everyone wants to be forgiven. Placing a child in the position of their parent being rated as a failure is not going to go down well with most children.

I watch as Alice's son now works with his child. I see many of his mother's parenting methods emerging as he loves and disciplines his child. Don't be afraid to put it in them. It will pay off in the end. Alice never said that she did not need a man to raise her sons. Rather than useless crying or man hating, she went ahead and placed them in her village for the vital help she needed. The village responded to the challenge and proudly can proclaim some more victories!

Two Kinds of Villages

It now occurs to me that there are two kinds of villages, and we need to talk about their differences. It is very popular to say, an old African proverb, *"It takes a village to raise a child"*. But we need to be aware that this statement may mean different things to different people. When the group I represent says it, we mean that we form an informal group of neighbors, friends, and church members, along with family members to look out for the welfare of a child or children that we know. Sometimes we are more selective and feel to narrow the group. For example, we may call for the church sisters to rally around a certain young lady who shows some tendencies toward unacceptable behavior. The sisters seeing this on their own without a called meeting may decide to speak to her one on one, or several at a time about what they are sensing. On the other hand, they may decide that they need to haul in 'Miss Out of Hand', into a more formal session. I feel somewhat sorry for the girl when this happens, because the sisters do not play, and can be rough! Anyway, it is all done in, and with, great love! The Bible even teaches us that, *"Whom the Lord loves He chastens"*. Can we who love our children afford to do less?

Often in this village if some finances are needed you will see individuals going into their pockets to make it happen. Many times, this will happen before there is a formal plea for any money. The village will tighten ranks and do whatever is needed. This is the nature of this village.

The makeup of our second village is very different in many ways. Make no mistake this village is very noble and quite serious about its devotion to the welfare and safety of children as well. Village two is made up, of not so much individuals, but mostly institutions, agencies and departments and manned by the individuals representing the protective philosophy to better the lives of children. These entities are usually much larger than the first kind of village we mentioned.

This second kind of village is comprised of all kinds of legal agencies that are placed in a mega net to protect and educate children. Schools, departments of Human Services, juvenile courts, police departments, custody courts, adoption and foster care agencies, and child placement agencies, to name a few. To back up these systems are all kinds of laws centering around prevention of child abuse and child endangerment. In harsh words, don't mess with our kids! Notice in the descriptions of this village there are words mentioned like, protection, provision, prevention, welfare, laws, and education.

Notice that missing from all of this is the word love. I'm sure that in the first village all of these things mentioned are of concern, but they are out ranked by the desire to love the child. The goal of village two is to provide for the safety and welfare of the child by marshalling every governmental force available in its network. Village number two is comprised of the government forces that will assure that its work will go on unhindered by any lack of structure. Many times, there is a giant overload and children somehow slip through the cracks. When there is a break-down somebody must be fired. It is the job of the big G to keep our children safe.

Often the problem is that in such a large development, children become faceless and fit in more like numbers than individuals. Love tends to be personal. A huge system does not have the opportunity or capacity to love. In fact, that's not even an objective!

STANDARD PARENTING 101

It does not matter if you are from before the "Silent generation" 1925-1945, the "Baby boomers" 1946-1964, or "Generation X" 1965-1980, or even "Generation" Y 1980-2000, or beyond: the same principles of parenting are in operation. God has placed the distinct assignment on parents to raise up their children according to the way they should go: spiritually, and individually. There is no special pass given. It is what parents are commanded to do.

This chapter is first of all about the standards—standards that do not change. Beginning with Proverbs 22:6 *"Train up a child in the way he should go, and when he gets old he will not depart from that training".* We see that this is not a suggestion! First comes the command and then comes the promise. Do this and the blessings will come. When we raise up our children with this twofold commandment, the outcome is that there is definite sticking power. The principles wrap themselves, actually knit themselves, to the very life structure of our children. In essence they cannot get away from them because they are a part of them. Now we all know stories of folks who were raised right and plummeted off of the deep end. The reality is these offspring are always haunted by what they know is right, even though they choose to do wrong. They cannot divorce their training. They may try to ignore it but they have to overdo to avoid it.

I met a man recently who kept telling me how much of a rebel he was. It was like he wanted to convince me that he was a real bad man. I also noticed that he was very respectful of my wife and me, and his mom who was present. We have been friends with his mom long enough to know that they come from an old Scottish-Catholic background. These folks don't play when it comes to rearing kids. Yet this fellow was trying hard to tell us that he had broken the mold. If he was all that bad, he would not care. He cared, because to me he was not all that bad! Now I recognize that he had been involved in some bad boy practices, but the fact that he had to try to distinguish himself away from being on the good side spoke volumes to me.

Some of the lessons to be taught

A journey beginning with the Psalms and on through to Proverbs will supply mountains of training information. I always greatly appreciate the teachings in Psalm chapter 1:1-6 that sets the stage by declaring that we be concerned about the benefits of our social environment: "*1 Blessed is the man Who walks not in the counsel of the ungodly, Nor stands in the path of sinners, Nor sits in the seat of the scornful*" . . . (paraphrased) Avoid walking in the counsel and false wisdom of the ungodly; don't hesitate by momentarily standing to contemplate sin; don't even pause to sit a spell with those who scorn and ridicule God and His wisdom.

You need to teach your child how to walk, stand, and sit while pleasing God, and in the personal formation of individual character. *2 But his delight is in the law of the LORD, and in His law, he meditates day and night.* Paraphrased: *It is wisdom to delight and find pleasure in meditating on the well proven law of the Lord.*

God gives His law as an ultimate blessing; never to curse you. In fact, there are great long term benefits to developing these character traits. *3 He shall be like a tree Planted by the rivers of water, that brings forth its fruit in its season, whose leaf also shall not wither; and whatever he does shall prosper.* Helping a child to discover the ways of God as he discovers his or her own way pays off. The analogy of a healthy tree drawing its nourishment from a companion river is priceless. The fruit is consistent and substantial, and whatever is done consistently within the life of that tree shall prosper. The scripture goes on to tell us:

> *4 "The ungodly are not so, But, are like the chaff which the wind drives away. 5 Therefore the ungodly shall not stand in the judgment, Nor sinners in the congregation of the righteous. 6 For the LORD knows the way of the righteous, But the way of the ungodly shall perish".*

This wonderful scripture should be encouraging and exciting for parents as they embark on this magnificent mentoring journey.

Honesty and integrity Psalm 19:14 *14 Let the words of my mouth and the meditation of my heart be acceptable in Your sight, O LORD, my strength and my Redeemer.*

This passage surely speaks about what comes out of the mouth as well as what lodges in the heart. So, we must teach our children to have clean and pure thoughts. Thoughts that produce positive actions. Even in the times of stress. Someone sent me a clip of a popular radio show where the nephew of the host called up an ailing deacon. The caller introduced himself as a new deacon at the church and was calling to pray for the elderly deacon who was about to have an operation on his pancreas. The spoof goes on as the caller begins to pray. He does very well in the beginning but starts mentioning healing for the old deacon's kidney. In the middle of the prayer he is stopped by the deacon who declares that there is nothing wrong with his kidney. *"In fact, my kidneys are very healthy"*. *"Really"*, said the caller? *"Then give me one"*. *"What"????* said the deacon. *"While they have you opened up"*, said the caller, *"you can give me your kidney, cause I need a transplant"!* Well, by now the elderly deacon begins to cuss up a storm. He says that this is the most outrageous call he has ever heard of. This caller is supposed to be calling to encourage him; instead, he is calling to solicit a kidney. The old deacon really loses it! When he is told that it was only a prank he was totally embarrassed. He said of himself that he had used language that he had not used for years. My point is that what is in will out. We should not blame the deacon for being angry; I think the best of us would be. The alarming thing is that he allowed himself to slip his discipline and began to act unlike who he was supposed to be in front of a large listening audience. Angry or not, the Word says, *"Let the words of my mouth and the meditation of my heart be acceptable in Your sight, O LORD, my strength and my Redeemer"*. And yes, I am not forgetting that God can forgive. Thanks be to God that His grace is amazing!

Integrity speaks to the quality of the product. I once preached a sermon entitled *'Will The Fabric Hold'?* The fabric of our lives must hold its consistency. We must teach our children to be consistent. Consistent in what they say, and consistent in what they do. One Saturday morning our two little children arrived home from their piano lesson. In their hands they held several beautiful tulips that they had picked for their mother. I asked them where they had gotten them. *"We picked them on the way home from music"*. Knowing that tulips do not grow wild in our community, I placed them in the car demanding they tell me exactly where they had picked them. I knew that the only place they could have gotten them was in somebody's yard. I was right. So, I took them back to the crime scene and made them apologize. *"Rash"*, you might say, but what was I doing? I was making sure that they knew that you cannot take other peoples' property. I don't think that after that embarrassing event they have ever touched anything that did not belong to them. The tulip owner was not very helpful as I recall. She thought it was cute that they wanted to do it to show their mother some love. But it was my job to make it a serious deed that was wrong!

We have got to teach consequences for actions. God holds us responsible for what we do. This is a fact of life. We cannot give our children false information because we don't want to hurt their tender feelings. Be the master teacher that God has assigned and equipped you to be. Never be afraid to instruct your children in righteousness. Again, one day, like the scripture promises, they will rise up and say you have been a personal blessing to them.

Respect and honor

One of my pet peeves in these times is the great loss of respect. There was a time when we did not even have to say respect your elders, your parents, other people's property, etc. Respect was just there. We did not even have to tell children and youth to respect themselves, they just did.

Speaking of consequences, has anybody taken notice that since the Supreme Court decision in 1963 to ban prayer in the public-school systems of the land that our children's respect level has steadily gone downhill? I'm not kidding, check it out. I think that you will be able to even document the decline. Check school behavior records. Follow that to see what the juvenile court records look like. There are those I'm sure who will tell you that it is all a coincidence. *Really??* I'm sure that there are many reasons for the decline but why can it be so dramatically traced back to 1963?

I came along in the generation before that dreadful decision was made. I will be quick to tell you that there was not that much prayer going on then. However, what sets my generation and those before that from 1963 is that we never had the audacity to tell God we didn't want Him in our schools at all. The system actually said to God that He was not welcome here. The day that God said, *"Goodbye"*, was sad for us! The court should have consulted God on the matter to see what He wanted to do with Madeline Murray O'Hare's lawsuit. God says in scripture, " . . . *a fool says in his heart that there is no God."* What our court system did not realize was that an official policy banning God from the schoolhouse was going to cause a real "Nor Easter." In our part of the country, it is a wicked storm that brews from several directions, mainly north and east causing all kinds of havoc in its wake.

Back in the day students used to respect their teachers. Next to their parents and minister the teacher ranked a close third. All of a sudden, things began to change. The old ways rapidly disappeared. Rebellion began to creep in almost everywhere. Property was no longer sacrosanct; it now represented the enemy. In many big cities, property was defaced with an awful vengeance. Paint spray cans, magic markers, crayons, nail files, and even lipstick became instruments of crime, as they scrolled, scrawled, scratched, and painted their boiling, seething new hatred for the faceless system. Almost simultaneously the dress code changed, and then all but disappeared. One school Superintendent said, *"I don't care how they come dressed, as long as they come covered."* And in today's scene that's about all many can look forward to; that they come covered! Students developed over the years an unhealthy and unholy disrespect for just about everything. This would include parents, teachers, administrators, policemen, judges, themselves, and yes even God! Their language often includes His name mingled among the vilest assortment of verbal filth. Youthful crime has risen to unparalleled highs. The drug culture has included in its clutches youthful offenders as far down as the primary grades.

The heroes for our kids used to be the folks who were positive role models in the community—folks who distinguished themselves in their careers, or put their lives on the line. After 1963 the heroes began to change. Drug lords, corner thugs and bandits took their place. Youth began to copy the dress codes of prison inmates who did what they did because of various prison situations. When belts were taken away from inmates for safety restrictions their pants sagged. Somebody on the outside thought that this was cool, and another fashion was born. *"Yucky do"*, I don't want to see your under shorts and beyond. All is not lost. We can change our sliding world, one child at a time. How? Go back to the old landmarks that were working. Teach them to our children. Hold the line when it is necessary. Pay attention to scriptures like Deuteronomy 19:14; and 27:17; also Proverbs 23:10 that give us insight about not moving old boundaries or landmarks. Take back territory that has been given away. Remember you are the parent. Don't be intimidated by your children. Go ahead repeat after me, *"I am the parent and this is my child (or these are my children). My children have been given to me by God to be raised with integrity"! "This I will do with all that is in me"!*

The Bible talks about the arrow maker creating strong and worthy missiles that are sent out as *His representatives*. Your children are your arrows. They represent God, and they represent you. Most likely what you teach to them, they will teach to theirs. We can change back to the standards if we take it child by child. The Bible instructs us *not to be weary in well doing*. Do what you can, trusting God and His Spirit to energize and magnify what you have invested. He will strengthen and keep you in perfect peace, but you have to keep your mind on Him and the task He places before you!

Good and Godly children do not manufacture themselves! The parent is strategically placed in a position to both instruct and to model that instruction. There are two old television commercials that come to mind. One I think was done by the lung cancer people. It showed a father and a little son hanging out together while the father was washing his car. He turns off the hose, reaches into his upper pocket, takes out a pack of cigarettes, takes one out and places the pack on the car hood. After lighting up he turns to see his little boy with one in his hand moving it toward his mouth. The father is horrified at what the little boy is doing. The camera fades to black. The message is pretty clear; *"What you do, they will do"*. The second commercial I'm not sure what they were selling but I remember it was after a snow storm. The father is walking through the deep snow and behind him are his children. Each of them is trying hard to jump into the tracks the father has made as they head to some destination. The message here is also pretty clear. The father is setting the path for his children.

Both of these were powerful visual messages made probably in the early seventies.

"What you do, they will do"!

Here are some additional important thoughts on *Training up the child . . .* Remember to work especially with your boys when it comes to the fine art of communicating. We tend to make our girls better communicators by the selection of toys we give them. We give them toys that evoke conversation skills. Dolls are good for little girls because they foster a kind of mother daughter connection. In that connection there is usually a kind of conversational piece going. The little girl will speak for herself and then for the doll. This might be both good and bad, as I think of it. Good because it teaches her that conversation should be two ways. Bad if it teaches her to carry on the conversation by herself. Speaking for the doll is one thing, but this will not work later in life when she has a husband. She will have to learn again, that B word, balance. She must learn not to become an over communicator. However, my point is that we usually furnish the little girls with things that represent some kind of verbal life—force. Dolls, stuffed animals, and things that represent life, aid in a communication experience as she grows up. If for instance, she has a tea set, she can use it to sit down and engage in imaginary conversation. Back in the day they used to have what they called "Doctor and Nurses sets". This again was a great toy for teaching empathy, emotions, and conversation, all of which most females excel at in life. Sometime a little girl could get her brother to play along for a minute, but since we were more prone to encourage our boys to be more athletic and energetic they would opt out for something more exciting and fast paced.

So, it is pretty safe to say that most of what our little girls are in touch with involves conversation. While she is putting her little doll down for an afternoon nap, instructing her stuffed animals to be on guard, her brother is in the next room having a completely different experience with his toys. He is playing with his Tonka truck, and his farm tractor while making the accompanying earth moving noises. Then on the other hand perhaps he has chosen to play with his Star Wars swords, or his hero action figures, all of which call for dramatic guttural sounds. Yes, he is indeed communicating, but without the use of good old standard word usage. He is missing normal human to human conversation. He is learning to create the grunts and groans, or the swishes and pow— pows that fit in with many of the masculine type toys that we supply. These provide hours of fun but do little to prepare him for the verbal side of life. Even when playing various sports the vocabulary can be extremely limited.

Ok, "Enough", you say! "What is the real point"? "So, boys have fun differently than girls; is that such a crime"? The real challenge for many men after they have grown up and get married is to shake off their boyhood practices of grunts and groans. They are quick to find out that their wives need to hear them using real valid words in making a connection. And not just a few words either. Either they learn that the grunts and groans of their past lives don't work and make the changes needed in this new domestic arena, or continue on in ignorance and frustration.

Then there is one more element that we recognize that occurs from the different backgrounds. Growing up, girls learn to talk and enjoy talking. In manhood, it is not that men can't talk. It is more like seeing the need and agreeing to talk. Sometimes, my wife will say something and my acknowledgement is, shall we say, just a little missing? *"Honey, did you hear what I just said to you? You didn't say anything"*. Now of course I heard her. We are in the same room and probably very close physically. Why wouldn't I hear her? The point is only from my male perspective: If we are in the same place, both with perfect hearing abilities, why in the world would I have to acknowledge that I heard you? Again, this is from that rather stupid male perspective.

Bottom line, let's agree to teach our male children the importance of learning to communicate and the great need to verbally communicate in life. This should be done on many levels and in many ways. This includes the toys that they play with. Mind you, I did not say that they can never play with trucks and tanks, etc. but I am saying that all things must be balanced out. We now realize that unintentional harm can come from ignoring how we teach and train our children in the early years. The outcome of this neglect may not show up until the grown-up years.

A BIBLICAL GUIDE TO PARENTING 101

H ere are some guiding scriptural references to help you on this wonderful journey of parenting. This guide of 14 selected ingredients is certainly not complete, but is intended to give you some quick scriptural references and comments. I have tried to place them into helpful categories. Because of biblical richness you may expect to see references fall into more than one subject heading.

Arrogance / Pride
Prov.3:26
For the LORD will be your confidence, and will keep your foot from being caught.

/ **Prov. 3:3-4**
"Let not mercy and truth forsake you; Bind them around your neck. Write them on the tablet of your heart, and so find favor and high esteem in the sight of God and man".

Heb.11:6
But without faith it is impossible to please (God) Him: for he that comes to God must believe that He is, and that He is a rewarder of them that diligently seek Him.

Try to teach your children to always be appreciative of who they are and what they have, but never to feel superior to others who may not have what they have. When God is gracious to us we must never feel that this puts us on a higher value scale than someone else. Children can easily feel that because they may have certain advantages over another child. Advantages can go away as fast as they can come. Teach them that little prayer insert that says, *". . . but for the grace of God, there go I . . ."!* Arrogance is a great sin before God.

Prov.16:18
Pride goes before destruction, and a haughty spirit before a fall. There once was a king who took great delight in showing off all his riches to a visiting king. He even exposed his visitor to his secret chambers. What he did not know was that he was setting himself up for a big overthrow. The invading king knew just where to go and what to look for. Arrogance is a great sin before God. Re-enforce the principle Prov.16:18 *pride goes before destruction, and a haughty spirit before a fall.* We should not think more highly of our selves than we do of others. This may prove hard to do when we have something that some others do not have, but remember it can be taken away almost in the twinkling of one's eye.

Avoiding Foolishness

Prov.4:14-17
"Do not enter the path of the wicked, and do not walk in the way of evil. Avoid it, do not travel on it; Turn away from it and pass on. For they do not sleep unless they have done evil; And their sleep is taken away unless they make someone fall. For they eat the bread of wickedness, and drink the wine of violence".

There is a difference in having fun and entering into foolishness. You will have to guide your child in the differences. Fun should never be at the expense of someone else's discomfort. We do not laugh at someone else's calamity. TV shows such as *"Jackass"*, are not funny, and in some instances have caused silly youngsters to try to duplicate bad stunts that go badly. Yes, sometimes we poke fun at someone but as soon as we see that it brings them pain, we should disregard that behavior. We learn in life to be sensitive to others. Why develop a joke, or make a comment that is character damaging to the point that it follows that person in their mind for life? It is surely not worth it. Teach sensitivity.

Hanging Out with the unscrupulous . . .

Prov.1:10-11
"My son if sinners entice you, do not consent. If they say, "come with us lie in wait to shed blood: Let us lurk secretly for the innocent without cause". Continue in **vv.15-16** *"My son, do not walk with them, keep your foot from their path; For their feet run to evil, And they make haste to shed blood".*

v.22 *"How long, you simple ones, will you love simplicity (naiveté)? For scorners delight in their scorning. And fools hate knowledge.*

/ **Prov.4: 17**
For they eat the bread of wickedness, and drink the wine of violence".

I did not always agree with my parents about hanging out with people who were different from us. I thought that they were being judgmental and exercising some kind of superiority thing. I knew quite well those old sayings, *'Birds of a feather flocking to gather'*, and *'one rotten apple spoiling the whole barrel'*, but I refused to see any relevance. Later, as I became wiser I understood that you just cannot hangout with people whose perspective is greatly different from yours. That old urge to belong, may be stronger than you think. It has pulled many people into its' web. Nobody wants to be thought of as an outsider. So even though there maybe barriers that are kind of sacred to the person, that old belonging to, fitting in thing, sometimes becomes the temptation that pushes them over the edge. Teach them to be leaders not followers! People who know who they are and do not have to find their identity in the life and misdeeds of others. There are countless people that have gone to jail, not for an actual crime that they personally committed, but because they were part of the mix. Teach your children to be independent enough in their thinking that if it comes to doing right or doing wrong, they will be able to choose what is right.

Honesty
Integrity

Prov. 3:3-4

"Let not mercy and truth forsake you; Bind them around your neck, write them on the tablet of your heart, and so find favor and high esteem in the sight of God and man".

Prov.3:26

For the LORD will be your confidence, and will keep your foot from being caught.

Prov.4:18

"But the path of the just is like the shining sun, that shines ever brighter unto the perfect day".

Psalm 1:1-6

1 Blessed is the man who walks not in the counsel of the ungodly, nor stands in the path of sinners, nor sits in the seat of the scornful; 2 But his delight is in the law of the LORD, and in His law he meditates day and night. 3 He shall be like a tree planted by the rivers of water, that brings forth its fruit in its season, whose leaf also shall not wither; And whatever he does shall prosper. 4 The ungodly are not so, but are like the chaff which the wind drives away.5 Therefore the ungodly shall not stand in the judgment, nor sinners in the congregation of the righteous. 6 For the LORD knows the way of the righteous, but the way of the ungodly shall perish.

John 8:12

Then Jesus spoke to them again, saying, "I am the light of the world. He who follows Me shall not walk in darkness, but have the light of life."

Integrity, like honesty is a choice. 'Back in the day', as they say, you could count on a man's word. The old timers used to say, *"You can set your watch on it"!* They also used another saying, *"A man's word is his bond"*. It is so interesting, that today you can hardly set anything on a man's word; and you certainly don't want to set your watch on him. I've observed in some of our city agencies, if they tell you that their closing time is 4PM, you best not call them after 2:45. They just will not answer the phones. They are preparing to go home at 4PM and your call might be more than they can handle in the 45minute period. So, my theory is that they just let the phones ring. Now I cannot prove this, but it does happen with frequency. I know someone who used to do temp work for one of the largest medical insurance companies. She said that in the department she worked in, there was a large stack of help needed letters from clients. In her spare time, she was trying to work down through the vast pile of requests and complaints. One day a supervisor saw what she was doing and told her to back off. She was instructed that they did not service that pile. So now you know what happens on the inside when it seems like you are being ignored. Yes, you are!

Have you noticed, that today there is almost no reliable guarantee on anything? What has taken the place of the guarantee is a warrantee. The written warrantee is made up largely, by a group of attorneys who have written into that document every form of why it is not their client's fault. Notice that products now often sell a beyond manufacturers' warrantee that runs along with the other warrantee. It is all designed to take as little responsibility as possible, and to maneuver out of being responsible for their product. I just believe that we have got to put integrity down deep in our children.

Intelligence / Education

Prov.3:26
For the LORD will be your confidence, and will keep your foot from being caught.

/ Prov.4:10-13
"Hear, my son, and receive my sayings, and the years of your life will be many. I have taught you in the way of wisdom; I have led you in right paths. When you walk, your steps will not be hindered, and when you run, you will not stumble. Take firm hold of instruction, do not let go; Keep her, for she is your life".

/ Prov.4:20-23
"My son, give attention to my words; Incline your ear to my sayings. Do not let them depart from your eyes; Keep them in the midst of your heart; For they are life to those who find them, and health to all their flesh. Keep your heart with all diligence, for out of it spring the issues of life".

John 8:12
Then Jesus spoke to them again, saying, "I am the light of the world. He who follows Me shall not walk in darkness, but have the light of life."

Intelligence and education from of old, started with the home. The scriptures indicate that it is the responsibility of the parents to teach and train their offspring in the very ways that they should follow. How you start them out is the likely path they will follow. My wife told me about an incident she overheard where my six-year-old grandson was lecturing his eleven-year-old Honor student cousin on one of C. S. Lewis' books. We laughed, but in reality, the boy devours a book before bedtime almost nightly. Often this is done while he is listening to his favorite children's Christian radio station. He does not seem to want to go to sleep without his routine. Years ago, there was a research study that showed college students did better academically when they read their Bibles regularly. These grades were contrasted against their previous grades during the time before they became Bible readers.

> **Prov.4:20-23**
> *"My son, give attention to my words; Incline your ear to my sayings. Do not let them depart from your eyes; Keep them in the midst of your heart; for they are life to those who find them, And health to all their flesh. Keep your heart with all diligence, for out of it spring the issues of life"*. This is the stuff good scholarship is made of.

Loyalty

> **3John4**
> *I have no greater joy than to hear that my children walk in truth.*

> **Jn.15:13**
> *Greater love has no one than this, than to lay down one's life for his friends.*

> **Luke 11:5-8**
> *5 And He said to them, "Which of you shall have a friend, and go to him at midnight and say to*

*him, 'Friend, lend me three loaves; **6** for a friend of mine has come to me on his journey, and I have nothing to set before him'; **7** and he will answer from within and say, 'Do not trouble me; the door is now shut, and my children are with me in bed; I cannot rise and give to you'? **8** I say to you, though he will not rise and give to him because he is his friend, yet because of his persistence he will rise and give him as many as he needs.*

Prov.18:24
A man who has friends must himself be friendly, but, there is a friend who sticks closer than a brother.

Loyalty is high on my list because that means we can count on each other. If I tell you that I am coming to your house to help you with something I feel that I am committed to do what I said I would do. I feel that applies to you as well. If you are my friend, I owe you, my loyalty. If you do something that I don't like, you are still my friend and I should not bail on you just because we do not agree. I watched on TV, a boyfriend and his girlfriend renovating a house. It started out in the beginning with the pledge of the two to make it happen together. I think that they were engaged to be married. I watched the poor guy put in all of his sweat equity, but the girl never showed up during the demo or the reconstruction. He needed her if for nothing else, moral support. Even the show host asked where she was. She just was a no show throughout. She did not demonstrate any loyalty. If it were me, I would have some second thoughts about marrying someone who said that they would help but never came to help with the load. What would marriage look like in their family? I recall that in our family we had a very famous celebrity who became a house whole name. Someone outside of the family was making a joke with one of the relatives about this celebrity. The relative did not find it funny at all, even though some of it might have been true. She simply replied tersely to the ridiculer, *"We don't talk about family"!* Her countenance showed that this outsider had seriously crossed the line. She demonstrated loyalty when she probably was in opposition to some of the things that the family member did. Yes, loyalty is big on my list.

Relationships

Matt.5:9
Blessed are the peacemakers: for they shall be called the children of God.

Matt.5:16
Let your light so shine before men, that they may see your good works, and glorify your Father.

Matt.6:2
When you do your alms (good deeds) do not sound a trumpet (or put on blast) before you.

Matt.6:14
If you forgive men their trespasses (failings) your heavenly Father will forgive you.

Prov.18:24
A man who has friends must himself be friendly, but there is a friend who sticks closer than a brother.

I think that most of the Bible centers on relationship building. Absorbing it gives one a sense of rightness when it comes to how to treat our fellow man. A neighbor is to be treated like we want to be treated. We are told to develop love for him in the same manner that we love ourselves. When Jesus teaches this interesting concept, we see that there are two major elements here. Both are of equal importance, and both are codependent on each other. In order to know how to love a neighbor there must be a healthy love for one's self. Not to be in love with ones' self; that's a real problem there. But if you do not love yourself, you would have absolutely no idea how to love me. If you loved me, and if it were even possible, to have absolutely no regard for yourself, it too would indicate some type of mental/spiritual illness taking place. God always urges balance in all things. So, a major factor in training up a child is teaching that child how to strive for a healthy balance. This is true in developing friendships, casual relationships, business encounters, family connections, and of course in marriages; actually, just life in general!

Reputation

Prov. 3:3-4
"Let not mercy and truth forsake you; Bind them around your neck; Write them on the tablet of your heart, and so find favor and high esteem In the sight of God and man".

Prov.4:*18*
"But the path of the just is like the shining sun, that shines ever brighter unto the perfect day".

Psalm 1:1-6
1 Blessed is the man who walks not in the counsel of the ungodly, nor stands in the path of sinners, nor sits in the seat of the scornful; 2 But his delight is in the law of the LORD, And in His law he meditates day and night. 3

He shall be like a tree planted by the rivers of water, that brings forth its fruit in its season, whose leaf also shall not wither; and whatever he does shall prosper. 4 The ungodly are not so, but are like the chaff which the wind drives away.5 Therefore the ungodly shall not stand in the judgment, nor sinners in the congregation of the righteous. 6 For the LORD knows the way of the righteous, but the way of the ungodly shall perish.

Prov.5:15
See then that you walk circumspectly, not as fools but as wise,

3John4
I have no greater joy than to hear that my children walk in truth.

Listen, there are not a whole lot of things to get bent out of shape over, but your reputation is one. Children must be taught the importance of a good name. You want to be who you say you are, and you want what they say you are to be accurate, and on point. There was a certain politician whose friend got into trouble. This politician was more concerned that his name not be linked with anything he felt that he was not involved with, than his friend's trouble. That's kind of harsh in light of what I have said about '*loyalty*', however I do understand what he was saying. *"Represent me as I am, not because of your expectation that so and so is my friend and because of that friendship, I must be guilty by association".* I recall walking into my classroom where a female teacher held her class during one of my free periods. It was the Christmas season and they were having a light hearted discussion about the coming holiday. I had to cross the front of the room in order to get to my little office. Her back was turned to me; and in response to their discussion, I wrote something funny on the black board just as I was ducking into my spot. The class laughed, getting her attention. To my surprise, she decided to come in the room and close the door behind her to make a comment. I'm sure you can imagine me backing her up out of there 90m.p.h. *'Hommie' don't play that for sure!!!* Well, let me tell you I could not wait to get to her later, to tell her not to ever let that happen again! She wondered why I thought the children would think anything was going on. Perhaps she was unaware that she did not have the best reputation to begin with. That shaky reputation notwithstanding, the principle would be the same. I fought hard not to ask her if she was nuts, or from another planet? Anyway, I felt that I had to go to war, if necessary, to protect that which I had worked so hard to build. People can feel like they know you, before they meet you because of what is said about you!

Righteousness

Prov.4:*18*
"But the path of the just is like the shining sun, that shines ever brighter unto the perfect day".

Psalm 1:1-6
1 Blessed is the man who walks not in the counsel of the ungodly, nor stands in the path of sinners, nor sits in the seat of the scornful; 2 But his delight is in the law of the LORD, And in His law he meditates day and night. 3 He shall be like a tree planted by the rivers of water, that brings forth its fruit in its season, whose leaf also shall not wither; and whatever he does shall prosper. 4 The ungodly are not so,

but are like the chaff which the wind drives away. **5** *Therefore the ungodly shall not stand in the judgment, nor sinners in the congregation of the righteous.* **6** *For the LORD knows the way of the righteous, but the way of the ungodly shall perish.*

3John4

I have no greater joy than to hear that my children walk in truth. Righteousness is, or should be, the sum total of how your personal character relates to others. We are taught, especially as Christians, that we should be a reflection of how God is. We must strive to do things the way Christ would be pleased. Someone tried to help us with that concept a few years ago with the W.W.J.D. (What Would Jesus Do) movement. It became a fad for a while, but the real strength of the slogan may have been lost to some. The purpose was to remind people to regard their daily walk according to the approval of Jesus. Righteousness should be a way of life, not some kind of bumper sticker, or badge we wear.

Self-Respect

Prov.3:26
For the LORD will be your confidence and will keep your foot from being caught.

Prov.4:20-23
"My son, give attention to my words; Incline your ear to my sayings. Do not let them depart

from your eyes; Keep them in the midst of your heart; for they are life to those who find them, And health to all their flesh. Keep your heart with all diligence, for out of it spring the issues of life".

Psalm 1:1-6

1 Blessed is the man who walks not in the counsel of the ungodly, nor stands in the path of sinners, nor sits in the seat of the scornful; 2 But his delight is in the law of the LORD, and in His law he meditates day and night. 3 He shall be like a tree planted by the rivers of water that brings forth its fruit in its season, whose leaf also shall not wither; and whatever he does shall prosper. 4 The ungodly are not so, but are like the chaff which the wind drives away.5 Therefore the ungodly shall not stand in the judgment, nor sinners in the congregation of the righteous. For the LORD knows the way of the righteous, but the way of the ungodly shall perish.

3John4

I have no greater joy than to hear that my children walk in truth. I think that self-respect goes along with the previous comments on reputation, honesty, and integrity, etc. When you are committed to doing what is right, and what is pleasing in God's sight, you can have joy in having a self-respect that is not mixed in with false pride.

Toxic Friendships

Prov.1:10-11

"My son if sinners entice you, do not consent. If they say, "Come with us lie in wait to shed blood: Let us lurk secretly for the innocent without cause". Continue in **vv.15-16** *"My son, do not walk with them, keep your foot from their path; for their feet haste to shed blood".* **v.22** *"How long, you simple ones, will you love simplicity (naiveté)? For scorners delight in their scorning. And fools hate knowledge.*

/ Prov.6:1-5

My son, if you become surety for your friend, If you have shaken hands in pledge for a stranger, 2 You are snared by the words of your mouth; You are taken by the words of your mouth. 3 So do this, my son, and deliver yourself; for you have come into the hand of your friend: Go and humble yourself; plead with your friend. 4 Give no sleep to your eyes, nor slumber to your eyelids. 5 Deliver yourself like a gazelle from the hand of the hunter, And like a bird from the hand of the fowler.

Prov. 2:12-15

12 To deliver you from the way of evil, From the man who speaks perverse things, 13From those who leave the paths of uprightness to walk in the ways of darkness; 14Who rejoice in doing evil, And delight in the perversity of the wicked; 15Whose ways are crooked, And who are devious in their paths";

Prov.22:24

Make no friends with an angry man, And with a furious man do not go, Parents must constantly monitor their children's friends. You are helping them not just for the present time but their future as well. You are teaching them how to choose the kind of people that will be good for them. There are people who will be like poison to them and others who will prove to be stable and sound. At the initial outset, most people will appear during childhood to be nice, and friendly, etc. but we know as wiser adults that we have to dive beneath the surface to discern the underlying character of the person. And we know that this is not always easy to judge. Often, we are fooled for awhile but in time most people will at some point come to the light enough that truth is revealed. Your children may not see what you see in helping them to move away from personalities that may in time prove to be toxic. Remember, even so, you are the parent. Your standard may not always earn you the popularity award from your children but that's ok, it is better to be right!

One of our girls had a girlfriend that seemed to have *'Trouble'* as her middle name. She was not so much her behavior on the surface, but under the surface she liked to venture into some on the edge thinking. After we discovered this about her, we had to try to gracefully discourage their close friendship. This was kind of hard, since the girls really cared for each other. If you put the good stuff into your children, they will begin to see those things that are not in their best interest. Our daughter did not like being in trouble. The other girl did not mind it at all. It was not too hard after a while for our daughter to make the decision. Even today, adults and cities apart, she will not have anything to do with this girl from her past. Then I remember one of our youngest son's schoolmates. His actions in front of us, were polite and mannerly, but underneath we could see thug written all over him. After he brought the residue of a gang fight into our rather quiet neighborhood, we did not have any trouble making the point about *unfriending* or *de-friending*, to use some Facebook terms, where our son was concerned. Put it into them and they will absorb it!

Truthfulness

Prov.3:9
"Honor the LORD with your possessions, and with the first-fruits of all your increase; so your barns will be filled with plenty, and your vats will overflow with new wine".

/ Prov.4:24
"Put away from you a deceitful mouth, and put perverse lips far from you".

Eph.5:15
See then that you walk circumspectly, not as fools but as wise,

3John 4
I have no greater joy than to hear that my children walk in truth.

We have to teach our children first of all that God is pleased with truthfulness. Truthfulness must be a way of life. In fact, I love the last part of 3 John4 ". . . *my children walk in truth*". It just ought to be the way we live. God requires it and God is it! You must train your child to be truthful. Surprisingly to some, your child does not come to earth naturally truthful and honest. Once a child realizes that there are negative consequences to messing up, they probably will lean toward covering it up. After that child finds out that there is also a penalty for lying about the mess up, as well as the penalty for the mess up, the pendulum may just shift toward telling the truth. Convincing your children to be truth tellers is a great character builder. From it will spring many positive virtues. Remember, there is always a balance to life.

We are not advocating the kind of behavior that uses truth as some kind of wooden club to bring pain to the heads and hearts of others. There are those people who feel compelled to tell everything they know. As I write this, our country is having a terrible time with a guy who somehow has commandeered a lot of sensitive intelligence documents and is in the process of releasing them to the world. He defends himself by saying he is releasing the truth that was done in secret. This is not only stupid reasoning, but also very dangerous. There are people's lives that are placed in jeopardy because of these secrets. How dare he uncover secret military defense sites, exposing our country and our allies to possible attacks. He has caused a firestorm in the diplomatic community as well. The only ones that are benefitted by this kind of information would be our terrorist enemies. My hope is they will charge him and all of his activist henchmen with treason! This is not truthfulness; it is big time treason in the sleaziest order. *"The truth is not to be known at all times!"* That's a quote from my grandmother.

Wisdom

Psm.111:10
The fear of the Lord is the beginning of wisdom . . .

/ Prov.1:5&7
A wise man will hear and increase in learning, and a man of understanding will acquire wise counsel. . The fear of the Lord is the beginning of knowledge, but fools despise wisdom and instruction

/ Prov.2:1-2
"My son, if you receive my words, and treasure my commands within you, So that you incline your ear to wisdom, and apply your heart to understanding";

/ Prov.3:5-8
"Trust in the LORD with all your heart, and lean not on your own understanding; In all your ways acknowledge Him, And He shall direct your paths. Do not be wise in your own eyes; Fear the LORD and depart from evil. It will be health to your flesh, and strength to your bones".

/Prov.3:13-18
"Happy is the man who finds wisdom, and the man who gains understanding; for her proceeds are better than the profits of silver, and her gain than fine gold. She is more precious than rubies, and all the things you may desire cannot compare with her. Length of days is in her right

hand, in her left hand riches and honor. Her ways are ways of pleasantness, and all her paths are peace. She is a tree of life to those who take hold of her, And happy are all who retain her".
Acts 5:29 *Obey God rather than man.*

Col.3:1-2
Set your affections on things above, where Christ sits at the right hand of God, and not things on earth.

Col.3:15-16
Let the peace of God rule in heart . . . Let the word of Christ dwell in you richly in all wisdom.

Prov.2:12-15
"To deliver you from the way of evil, From the man who speaks perverse things, From those who leave the paths of uprightness To walk in the ways of darkness; Who rejoice in doing evil, And delight in the perversity of the wicked; Whose ways are crooked, And who are devious in their paths";

Perhaps one of the greatest ways to teach your children wisdom is using the Proverbs reading plan. Nothing like rocket science; just put them on a regular daily calendar routine. That's it; read the book of proverbs according to the date. There are thirty-one books of Proverbs. So at the end of most months, you have read thirty one. Those months that have less than thirty-one you can be creative in how to handle those. Wisdom will seep in as they read these wonderful passages that are packed full of timeless gems month by month, year by year. I had some surgery recently that required them putting me to sleep. They hooked me up to an IV bag that supplied a constant drip. How in the world was this slow drip going to make a difference in my state of being? I kept waiting for them to put a mask on me that would sedate me so that we could get this surgery on. The next time I was realizing life, was when they were waking me up. That steady drip took me out of all conscientiousness. This is how a steady dripping of the scripture will make its' mark on the recipient.

There you have it—my list of fourteen principles that must be taught to our children. These, as I began this chapter, are not the only things that have to be taught to them but make up the basis of the learning pool. If you can guide them along these principles, you will notice that the way will open to them to incorporate other guiding principles. **Never forget you are the parent! God holds you responsible for the guiding of your children, from infancy to the beginning of adulthood!** You dare not try to raise them over again after they are grown. You may have advice to share but always remember they are now grown people. Respect them as you would any adult. Sharing is not a bad thing but must be done with respect and great balance. Then know that after you have had an opportunity to share your wisdom it is still up to them whether they choose to follow your sharing. I believe if you have raised them properly, they will not go too far afield in their practicing. If you did not raise them correctly, oh well, that's going to be an uphill battle. Perhaps you can make some headway by being a demonstration of the things that you have been learning in your post parenting times.

Carl was a terrible example during the parenting years. It was almost like his business was more important to him than his children. It wasn't until he retired that he realized that he had put his children in a kind of isolation. They felt almost no love from him as they grew up. His wife tried to tell him but he was just not interested in making any changes in his life-style. I think it took the Lord to get through to him. Maybe it was after his sudden illness, or his new found faith in God that helped him begin to realize that he needed them, and that they were starved for a relationship with him. No matter how it happened, he changed. Even though all of his children were grown with their own children, the love and concern he began sharing with each of them, melted the cautions between them. Now these days they eat up every word of wisdom he shares. He has not tried to force anything on them, but just started practicing that which he failed to teach in the formative years. So, I guess that it is never too late to line up with biblical principles. Rev. Dale Oldham sang a Bill Gaither song with loving and inviting words: *" The longer I serve Him, the sweeter He grows; the more that I love Him, more love He bestows. Each day is like heaven, my heart overflows; The longer I serve Him, the sweeter He grows."* I wanted to stop but allow me one more verse: *"Since I started for the kingdom, since my life He controls. Since I gave my heart to Jesus, the longer I serve Him the sweeter He grows . . ."* To some this may seem a little simplistic, but the reality is that it does work, and work well! The longer you go in a certain pattern the more that pattern becomes a part of you. This principle works either way. It works in those positive things we reinforce as well as those negative things we practice.

PARENTING: SOME OTHER THINGS I KNOW...

These are things that come to mind in no particular order, but will prove helpful if you keep them in mind and find ways to give them practice!

Every kid is unique...

Raising children should be, over all, fun! It is both a learning opportunity and a growing opportunity for both the parent and the child. In some ways all children are alike, but in many ways they are different. They are more than likely different even when raised in the same household. So, the astutely gifted parent must figure out the differences as they go along. It was interesting watching our two oldest children growing up. They seemed to be pretty much alike in temperament and behavior. But we realized that as they grew more mature they began to develop some individual differences. They both chose the same profession and took similar courses of study in college and graduated with degrees in communication. One surged full speed ahead into a career in journalism, the other just as gifted applied the brakes because of the personal discovery that there was a lack of aggressive skills and temperament needed for success in that area.

It is ok for your children to be different. I pointed out earlier in this work that the Bible says to train up a child in the way that he/ she should go and they will not depart from that training. Put the good stuff in them and they will sort it all out later. Don't stress it, they are supposed to be different.

Relax and enjoy them!

"You are going out of here..."

Laughing, I remember those words of my father when I declared one day that I wasn't going to school because I didn't feel like it. My Dad. A man of few words, always seemed to come up with a memorable phrase that pretty much punctuated the moment. Anyway, in thinking about that phrase I want to say to parents in this highly technical society, be mindful that your child needs sunshine. A recent study pointed out that many of today's young are vitamin D deficient. Vitamin D comes largely from the sun. To get full exposure to the sun you have to be outside of the house. Now the problem is that our children are so enmeshed in computer stuff that they don't have to go anywhere. They have I 'pods, I 'phones, lap tops, Tablets, Xboxes, on and on. Because of the wonderful virtues of the internet, Wi Fi, and who knows what tomorrow will bring, they can be sitting at the kitchen table and be transported to China, or Africa, or to a local sports stadium without moving their chair. But that's the point! They need physical exercise, and they need vitamins from the elements out of doors.

When I was growing up, even for a city kid, I got plenty of fresh air. In the summers, when school was out, I spent much of my day in the park playing baseball. Almost like clockwork, I would mount my bike with my trusty glove, put a bat on the handle bars, and take off for Strawberry Mansion Park. It was my week-day ritual. From morning to dusk I was there. Funny, I must have eaten lunch, but I don't even recall that. What I do recall is the times when we had a break between games, riding down to the spring and lapping up that cool clear water pouring from the rocks. To me, these were the good times that etched themselves into my memory for life. These were real events - not virtual! I can still see, in my mind, the times when we looked across the vast fields to see a rain storm sweeping towards us, giving us a few seconds to race for some kind of shelter. Since we were in the park there was very little shelter so we mostly got wet. But then the Sun would find its way back again to dry us as we played some more ball. Wow, you see what I am talking about? Real memories, are still there, and still alive! This virtual stuff is not real. I wonder what our technocratic children will have to look back on when they are old.

Oh, and I know all that I said about being in doors too much, but there needs always to be a balance. Find ways to stimulate and challenge the brain as well. The computer stuff is good for the grey matter. It is mostly how, and when, you use it. Always monitor the technology that your children are exposed to. I think they really should have access to these things, just not all the time, and everything. Balance, balance, balance!

I know your child is amazing, but stop stressing yourself... Some have called it Mom's taxi or the Dad route. It is when you think that wonderful child of yours needs to be a star triple sports athlete, science fellow, Rhodes Scholar, artist, and academician.

Relax, stop running yourself ragged. Your wonderful child will likely still be wonderful. I know parents who have tried to enroll their children in just about everything in the world that presented itself as an opportunity. They took on one of our former presidents' sentiments of *"No child left behind"!* They took it as a personal message and challenge designed especially for their family. Trust me, he was not talking to your already over extended crew!

You are killing yourself for no good reason. Diane said, *"I will not let my child come behind in anything".* Ok, so she has him enrolled in T Ball, swimming, pre-track and field, and Karate. When one event, or practice is over she has to spirit him away to the next thing. They have a ridiculous calendar on their kitchen wall with all of the events, practices, meetings, and whatever else they can fit in. STOP the madness! You cannot possibly do everything and be everywhere! Relax, that special child will still be alright even if you elect to calm down on the enrollments and activities.

I would rather see a child be allowed to concentrate on one area that they really like and be consistent in it than running all over everywhere mastering nothing, and not having any fun doing it anyway. And throughout all of this madness the parents get burned out as well! So, I say relax; if you put the proper training in them they will make out fine.

Unhealthy sibling rivalries are a no - no...

In our house we did not allow our children to fight, aggressively argue, or name call. Some would say that we were not equipping them for the real world. What I say is, we were equipping them to help solve the real world. We taught them to know their point of view and then to stand on what they believed, without having to get out of character to defend it. The little slogan that I drilled into their heads and hearts is that, *"The man who has the experience is never at the mercy of a man who merely has an argument"!* So with that, they have each learned to be great debaters. They keep their cool and point always to the subject at hand, and never insult their opponent. Why lose your head, or a friend, over a silly difference of opinion? We taught them that family should be close. Your siblings should be, and can be, your friends. Work at it, it is worth it in the long run. Today they are all good friends. It gives me great pleasure to know as adults they genuinely love each other. We worked hard at it as parents; but now comes the payoff. You see the secret is this, if you can learn in the house how to build good solid relationships, you can take that same method out into the world where relationship building is so needed, but so lacking!

Shooting wooden crows off a wire fence...

Well, here is something my mama taught me. I was having one of those moments while growing up. I just didn't seem to be able to make friends in the neighborhood, to put it mildly. My parents had rules that some of the other kids found ridiculous. Because of that, they made fun of me and it was getting me down. Laboring over the thought that I was destined to go through life having almost no one like me was weighing me down. I think I may have been crying over it one day when my wise mom stepped in. She asked me about that game I was playing with the day before. The one with the black crows on the wire fence and the cork gun. Oh, right away, I told her the name of the game and she told me to bring it to her. I thought to myself, I'm having trouble with my social life and my mom wants to play this game. She told me to take it and set it up on the front door steps. What craziness was this? People already don't like me and think I'm weird and now she wants me to set up this stupid game on my front steps where the whole world will come by and see me shooting black crows off of this wire fence. Why would any mother put her child in that predicament? There I kneeled in shame, popping crows with my cork gun. Out of the corner of my eye I saw the figure of the kid from 3 houses down watching me. It seemed like he was inching closer (*I was sure to be the star of a good laugh*) and before I could fully appreciate my humiliation he asked me what I was doing and could he have a turn. Well, this little kid who never liked me, wanted to play with me because I was doing something interesting. Thank you mom, now up in heaven! You taught me one of the greatest lessons in winning friends. Just do what you do - have fun doing it, and someone will come along and want to join you in doing it!

"Go in a haste - come in a pace..."

My hard-working dad, who I believe could not read or write very much was one of the smartest guys I've known. Dad didn't talk much, but when he spoke people listened. I listened! When he would send me to the store on Susquehanna Avenue he often would say, *"Go in a haste and come in a pace"*. Well, I knew that meant not to stop on the way to or fro! He taught me to always be about business. If you didn't have any business, always look like you have some. Don't stop by the way because that's where trouble lurks. So, from there I learned to never hang out on corners, my business was at home.

Ha ha hah ha, I remember on my way to the Avenue I had this imaginary stallion (*don't recall the name*) but anyway as I journeyed on I would break into this gallop that simulated riding my horse. I would vary the speed from a slow trot to a pretty full gallop depending on the mission. Now that I think back, I really had so much fun on these journeys. Sometimes it was to the butcher, or the drug store, or some other business for my folks. My trusty horse was always waiting for me outside the store for that welcomed ride home. Gee, now that I think back I wonder what the neighbors must have thought. Here is this kid who always ran pass in a type of horse gallop holding imaginary reins. Hmm, what must have been going through the neighbor's minds? But anyway, thanks dad, I never took the time to be idle because you taught me to *go in a haste and come in a pace,* smile!

There was always a lot of laughter in our house...

I recall a discussion among some of my gifted students in my high school classroom one day. Several of them were talking about the Cosby Show on TV. Some of them said that the show was not real life. The kind of antics featured were not how families acted. I said to them that it was exactly how our family acted; lots of fun and frolics. Often, I was the fall guy, or the one who had to straighten out something or another, but most of the time, crazy fun!

Our kids always had a production of some kind going on. Mike was always finding ways to do a newscast or practicing doing the weather. This sprung from his early days of taking ham radio at the community center. His love propelled him into that career. Shana also loved communications but leaned more towards the dramatic areas. We discovered that Faith was the comedian of the family and David Paul was some of all the above. Being the youngest, it was hard to figure out where he was really going to land. He would tell us that he was going to enter a rap contest the next day at the center and planned to win. We'd never heard him rap or even listen to rap, but needless to say he walked off with first prize. And who can forget the day when we were sitting around laughing and talking, and 10 or 12 year old D.P. walked by the family dressed up in my long raincoat and big hat, somebody's oversized eye glasses and a briefcase announcing that he was going down the street to get a job. We were speechless as he disappeared out the door and across the porch. What a sight! So, you see there was always something that kept us rolling on the floor!

We had fun shooting scenes and then watching all the family video productions, listening to music, pulling pranks, family debates, and such wonderful crazy fun times. When the Cosby program came along on TV, it was just like what we were used to in our home.

Our children loved to play board games too. You can actually see some character traits emerging and forming in how participants play games. Actually, in any kind of game, but very much in board and table games. I guess this is because you are sitting in close proximity to players. One of the favorites of the kids was Monopoly. You kind of got a sense of the deep-down stuff in a person's character. We had a neighbor who you would have thought was investing real money. He was so intense that it was a little scary at times. This told us a lot about the aggressive figure crouching inside of him.

Gifts making room for them…

The Bible teaches us that a person's gifts will make room for him/her. We taught our children to work hard at what they did, make sure they did it well and then leave the results to God. Now that sounds easy, but you really have to understand it, and then grow into it.

I learned something from my late friend James Jefferson during the intermission of a concert. I remarked about some people we observed who always seemed to be hawking their talents. Every time you saw them they seemed to be campaigning for a spot on a program or something. Jeff agreed that their pushy behavior was a little over the top, but he added this: *"If God gives you a talent to be shared, do you think He wants you to hide that talent until someone accidently trips over you and discovers you have it"?* Wow, after that I never looked at that scripture in the same manner. He was right; it should not always be by discovery by accident! Allow people graciously to know that you have something to share if they should ever need you. Don't, however, hem people up in a corner choking them to death. I do believe a person's gifts make room for them to share them. Stuffing them in on people is rude, and then not allowing others to share theirs because of yours, is arrogant. God gives us gifts to be a blessing in the kingdom; not to stroke an out-of-control ego!

Finding a balance between allowing people to know that you have a talent that you are willing to share, and not being pushy and blatant, is a bit tricky. But remember again, scripture teaches that your talent or gift will make a place for you. There is the song that says *He does not teach us to swim so that we can drown,* etc. If God gives you a song, there is an audience of one or more that wants, and needs, to hear that song!

Teach your children the value that God has placed on all of His children; them included. Teach them respect, appreciation and humility. Teach them preparedness, willingness, and appropriateness.

One interesting Christmas…

My wife and I were laughing the other day about the time our Mike got into trouble a few days before Christmas. I don't remember what he did but we had to come up with a punishment. I decided to make him work to find his presents. I carefully worked out for us an elaborate kind of treasure map of where I had hidden all of his gifts, and designed all of the clue cards that would help him find them. So early on Christmas morning instead of his gifts being under the tree like everyone else, Mike got a card telling him to go to a certain spot for the next clue. Honestly, I ran that boy all over the house with these clues. He loved it! What started out as punishment turned out to be fun for him! In subsequent years he begged us to hide his presents and do the search game again. I don't remember *punishing him* like that again. Too much work! I think the joke was on us! And of course, the others wanted to be punished too!

Guard your secret ingredients...

I have always been a very creative person. Often, full of ideas and dreams. There have been times that these ideas have struck a resonant chord in the minds of others who figured that the idea was free for the taking. So, as I wandered through life I found out that it was not always good to share it all with everyone. Yet in order to get some things started in life, a part must be shared. There is an expression I think came from government sources that says *"On a need-to-know basis"*. Well, what I taught my children is to learn to hold out that thing that will cause your idea to work in its best way. That secret ingredient that will cause the magic to work belongs only to you! Companies like Coca Cola, Bush's Baked Beans, and others do not disclose their secret ingredients that make their product unique. Even Pepsi does not taste just like Coke because they supposedly don't know the secret formula of their competitor.

Teach your children how to honestly duck and dodge not giving away the thing that makes it work, and not feel guilt for holding it back. Sometimes people will try to make you feel you are not being friendly when you are not taking them into your confidence, but guard your secret anyway. In the end the credit should go to the creator of the idea not the one who merely copies. Trust me, I have learned this firsthand.

One example I'll share is when I was teaching secondary art classes. I came up with an idea to develop a series of video lessons centering on learning to do an oil painting. There was a School Board meeting in our building that I did not attend. Someone knew about my work and they got my friend the A/V man to pull out and show the files. My supervisor was there and became very interested. I got a call from him the next day. He wanted me to share the information of what I was doing with a senior art teacher in another school so that he could make the video series. This man was well known in the School District of Philadelphia and I was not. Like they say, *"I was born in the daytime, but not yesterday"*, smile!

Teach them not to cave in from pressure. My boss had a lot of power but I didn't feel that he had the right or ability to make me give up my creative properties. He was only my boss, not my owner. Teach them to guard their integrity while they are guarding their things. Your children must learn to be truth-tellers in spite of what it looks like. I recall a secretary being instructed by a boss to say that he was not in. She told her boss that she did not lie for herself so she could not lie for him. *"I can say that you said you were not in"*. At that, the boss promptly answered the call and never asked her to lie for him again. Make personal integrity a personal must!

Teach your children to be big dreamers...

Dare to dream big; that is the vehicle that will transport them from the common place to the rare. The Bible instructs us in this concept when it says, *"Without a vision the people perish"*. Another saying I remember hearing is that, *"if you aim at nothing the reward is predictable, you'll hit every time"*!

I believe that there are fewer dreamers in the population than ordinary folks. There is nothing wrong with you if you are not a dreamer. I think that statistics would show dreamers to be in a small minority group, but I believe it can often be an underappreciated group too! If your child is leaning toward being a creative thinker or dreamer you are going to have to teach him/her how to be strong and encouraged when rejected by others who simply don't understand. I was often put down and rejected while growing up. No, I was not strange or crazy as some might have supposed. After a few disappointments I figured it out. If you want people to continue to like you, the best way to introduce your dream is to ease it in slowly. Dumping it on them is not a good idea. There are some, not a massive number, who will listen and really get it. The big mistake dreamers make is that we feel everyone is going to jump on board with us. That rarely happens. The more natural way is that a very small few may catch on to what you are talking about. Later, a few others may come to it. Once the idea really takes off there will be another group who buy in. This is probably the way most new, or novel ideas get off of the ground, but that's alright. What parents have to do for these children is to prepare them to push on through, without having a majority of followers. They must learn to go for it whether they have everybody or nobody! Teach them to trust God, believe in themselves, look out at the field of need and possibility, test the market, and make the advance! These are the basic lessons to help your dreamers to be equipped for success. One more thing is needed: prepare them to understand that you can have the perfect idea and it still might not fly.

While you are at it you might teach them the art of changing up. Another mistake that some dreamers make, is not knowing when and if changes to the original idea need to be considered. Before an idea that seems to be going down in defeat happens, there may be some surgical changes that will save it. I don't like what I call desperation changes, but many times some well thought out changes are in order.

Invest in their big dreams...

I do thank God for the life of Eugene Stevens. My dad was not very talkative but he was an encourager. I don't think he ever told me no when I wanted to venture out on something.

I remember when I wanted to own a car at sixteen, he found a mechanic who had a 1938/39 Chevy for sale. I wanted to buy it and they arranged for me to start making payments from my earnings until I was able to purchase it and drive it home. Notice, he did not buy it for me, but allowed me to know how to pay for my dream. He taught me how to be responsible and how to finance my dream at the same time. Now he could have said to me that I was too young to have the responsibility of owning a car, etc. but instead he guided me into ownership. He did not do it for me, so to speak, but rather, he acted as a facilitator. He encouraged me to learn how to do the maintenance on my car. Once I remember he helped me rebuild the engine in my grandfather's garage. This of course was when engines were pretty simple. I don't think I would attempt that particular task today with these complicated machines. The day I noticed that the engine in my Nissan was turned sideways was the day that I decided that I didn't have the skills to go much further than changing oil, light bulbs, and batteries, and supplying the fuel.

"Mr. Eugene", as he referred to himself sometimes, was strong but mostly silent, not in a creepy way, but he just would not talk on and on like some folks do. He was interesting when it came to sharing things from his past. He liked to sum up what he was thinking in as few words as possible. He never told jokes as I recall but was often funny without trying to be. I remember we were painting the back of a ladie's house together, when I looked back and remarked from the ladder how far down it was. He did not miss a beat, saying it was not the long distance down that would kill you, but the quick stop!

Now to be fair, I should mention that Emma Stevens was my dream supporter too. She, was like the warm blanket that covered me. She always found a way to bring me comfort, especially in those times of stress. Once, I was working on a model car for a competition and the paint can tipped over on me, the car, the floor and everything. I was so frustrated that I opened the basement door and was about to throw it down into dark forever, when my mother came behind me and grabbed my hand assuring me that it all could be cleaned up. In my moment all I wanted to do was end the project. I was undone and saw no other way. Mom was a quick thinker. She knew that I would come to regret later, a very hasty decision to end my dream. Most of the time one can recover from an accident if you don't compile insult to injury. Yes, Emma Stevens taught me many lessons that have carried me through life. She encouraged me to be a dreamer and to stick to the dream.

When your child shares a dream with you don't take over that dream but help them to begin developing that dream. They will need to put together some kind of planning for it to work. Help them develop not only the main plan but an alternative plan as well. You are teaching them some skills for life. In their own way they taught me to never give up. Just like Sir. Winston Churchill, *"Never, never, never give up"!*

"Go to church..."

I say this all the time! My congregation might be tired of hearing it but it is right! I think if we took a survey, we would find that children that are raised in church, overall do better in the flow of life than those who do not attend. I don't have facts and figures at hand to prove my theory, but just general observation. Children raised in church generally have a better perspective on personal faith, hope and love. This is not odd because these are some of the things that the teachings of the church center on. I believe that the central teachings of Jesus when understood supply the tools of life. The church should be teaching and reinforcing these life tools for all they are worth.

Back in the early days of our church I believed it was my duty to not only teach the adult population the rudiments of the gospel, but strive to break it down so that the children would learn too. I felt that it was the duty of the pastor to get through to the little ones along with the others. So much so that I fought against having children's church for years. I only relinquished when I became convinced that the team could do it better. They could do it better because educating the children became their total focus as opposed to my focus on feeding everyone. But rest assure, my passion is still with the children. Maybe that's the teacher in me. Church, when done right, should be instilling the life principles that are going to equip children for their entire lifetime!

Principles, morals, philosophical/theological concepts are all things that should be taught in the church. Some reactions to life ought to come as second nature to us because of our grounding in church teachings. One of the glaring things that I note in observing so many of todays out of church youth is the loss of respect for human life. In the news we hear of so many who will fight over, and even kill over, nothing. The church teaches the value and importance of every life. The great out-there teaches things like, *every man for himself, the survival of the fittest,* and *kill or be killed.* Foolishness at its worst. I remember when I was teaching in high school seeing two boys planning to fight after school. I tried to talk to them individually about not letting this thing go to that end. I knew the boys were not planning to get into an old fashioned fist fight. So, I pleaded with each to make peace because it was over some dumb thing that was not worth their time. I remember the one boy, whom I liked a lot, saying to me, *"Doc, don't get caught in a crossfire".* He was warning me that he cared about me and that he would hate to see me shot trying to break up something that I was powerless to prevent. I recall feeling that emptiness in the pit of my stomach as I had to resign to that same moment of helplessness and hopelessness.

Take them to church! Church is where God can enter their thoughts and challenge them to live real life to its' fullest. Church is the place where the real village can help you raise your children. The brothers and the sisters become the strong community that will aid your efforts as a parent. Thank you, Pastor Allen Mack, Mother Rouse, Sis. Spencer, the Richardsons, Bros. Raymond and John Gary, Sis. Willa Mae Gary, and Sis. Juanita Jones all from The Community Church of God. Thank you, Brother and Sis. Tom Baxter, Pastor Elsa Bass, and Pastor Dan Burnside, from Christ Center Church of God. These are just a few of the many people that helped to impact our children as they grew up in the church. I am very happy to report that each one of our children and their families are still fully functioning somewhere in the church today. Thank you, God for teaching us that concept, *"…That as for me and my house we will serve the Lord".*

Teach them to read and honor the Bible as God's word. Teach them how to pray and communicate with God. Surround them in the hymnology of the church music, even if later they develop interest in other types of music, the lyrics of that strong hymnology will stick in their souls.

Tell them your stories…

I remember, it was Brother Burnside, my dad, and a couple of other men standing with me in the rear of the church, after service, telling old childhood stories to each other. We were all having a great time of it when I noticed an outer ring of mostly boys, but some girls too, listening to us and enjoying it with us! This was not a formal anything, just some guys enjoying each other. But what I discovered is that children and youth still enjoy listening to the stories about the things that we found delight in. This was many decades ago, but I've seen it over and over again. We need to share our past with our children!

One of the desperate things I see today is the lack of a communication effort between age groups. Don't be afraid to tell them about the good, the bad, and the sometime ugly. It is a sad commentary that so many youngsters today have absolutely no idea about the lives of their parents as children. Their sense of history is so limited, it's a shame. Maybe it is because of the busy pace we find ourselves in, or perhaps it is our love affair with technology via. Iphones, computers, tablets, etc. Gadgets have actually stolen family time. It is interesting that the communication inventions and gadgets have actually been the source of communication disruption.

Take time to talk to your children. Tell them your stories of the past. Share with them how you grew up. They need to know about the things and events that made you, you! I remember my mom telling me about the time she was sitting on the porch back in her days in the old South. She was a pre-teen sitting there throwing seeds at a young man passing by in the yard. She was disciplined by a family member because in those times she was considered being fresh. It was just a funny little occurrence but it highlighted the differences in culture from her time to mine. Today, over sixty years since I heard it, it would only appear as a blip on the radar of importance. But look, it is still in my thoughts. It is part of a treasured memory of something my mother told me.

Don't be afraid to tell them truth through your stories. They will be able to see it long after the time in which you tell them. Stories implant living pictures on the walls of the mind. Pictures that remain. I learned some of this by listening to my friend the late Rev. Dr. Pastor Horace Wesley Sheppard Sr. Pastor Sheppard, especially as he got older, used to interject such fascinating stories in his sermons. The stories almost became the messages. The audience could often get so involved that you would hang on every word. Well, I just thought that was the coolest thing. So,

I began doing it also. It is alright to become a yarn spinner of sorts. Your children will not easily forget what you have taught them through this method. Later, I discovered that there was a study that showed that this is the way to win men in particular, because men love hearing stories. **And guess what, JESUS DID IT that way!**

YOUNG DAVID & DOROTHY EVENTUALLY MEET AND MARRY.

WE ARE FAMILY OF 6

MIKE (the first born)

OUR EXTENDED FAMILY

FAMILY LOVE AND JOY

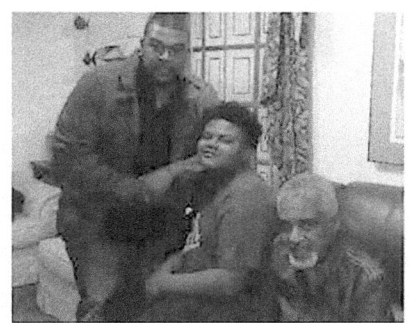

NOTHING BEATS THE LOVE AND JOY FROM YOUR FAMILY

EVERYDAY FEELS LIKE A CELEBRATION WITH THEM

STILL IN LOVE

"some of the most important things in the world are love, family, and being good parents."

David R. L. Stevens, D.D.

Rev. Dr. David R. L. Stevens is a graduate of Anderson University. He is the founder and senior pastor of Christ Center Church of God in Philadelphia, PA and has served the congregation for the past 52 years. He was ordained on September 14, 1969 by the Church of God, general offices in Anderson, IN, and received his Doctor of Divinity Degree on June 6, 1981 from the Jameson College in Philadelphia, PA.

Before retiring from the School District of Philadelphia, Dr. Stevens taught in the Mentally Gifted Program. He currently serves as the Chairman of the Delaware Valley Pastor's Fellowship which started November 1969 and consists primarily of 25 senior pastors, and their associates, within the tri-state area: Philadelphia, New Jersey and Delaware. Dr. Stevens also serves as Chairman of the Credentials Committee for the Church of God in the East, District 41. He is a professional artist, a marriage counselor, and has authored eleven books on the subject of marriage and relationships: <u>Marriage: Castle, Corridors, and Conflicts</u>; <u>Marriage: The Rules of the Game</u>;

Marriage: Catching a Second Wind; Love, Marriage and the Baby Carriage; Falling Back in Love; and Falling Back in Love Again; Love Marriage and Your Kids. He is in the process of publishing a two-volume book under one cover: Love and Marriage for A Lifetime. Add to that, to be released at the same time, a 3rd book in that series; PARENTING: Equipping Babies for A Lifetime. Dr. Stevens has also authored 3 online books: LOVE FOR A LIFETIME; MARRIAGE FOR A LIFETIME; and EQUIPPING BABIES FOR A LIFETIME. He has produced various sundry videos and publications. Each week he faithfully sends out scores of email sermon outlines called Mail-A-Messages to an online congregation. He has also opened up a cyber counseling ministry through Facebook and the https://drstevenssoundmarriages.com/ website where people can get relationship counseling anonymously.

Dr. Stevens is married to Mrs. Dorothy Grimball Stevens, and together they have four children all actively serving in the church, and 10 grandchildren and two great-grands. They co-founded the Second Wind Second Mile Ministries, now known as "Sound Marriages" over 40 years ago. Their marital philosophy is, *"Making good marriages even better."* Dr. & Mrs. Stevens have traveled nationwide doing seminars, presentations, workshops, and private counseling sessions, sometimes at their own expense. They say, *"Because we love God and His people"!* Website info: https://drstevenssoundmarriages.com/